FOR THE LOVE OF AN EAGLE

JEANNE COWDEN

FOR THE LOVE OF AN EAGLE

David McKay Company, Inc.
New York

To the memory of my parents, Ida Mary and John,
who gave me a priceless gift—their
love of the wild.

First American Edition, 1976

Library of Congress Cataloging in Publication Data

Cowden, Jeanne.
  For the love of an eagle.

  SUMMARY: A South African woman describes her experi-
ences during the filming of a family of eagles in the
Drakensberg Mountains.
  1. Aquila verreauxi—Legends and stories—Juvenile
literature. [1. Eagles] I. Title.
QL795.B65C68 1976   598.9'1   75-43023
ISBN 0-679-20304-4

MANUFACTURED IN THE UNITED STATES OF AMERICA

Acknowledgments

I am grateful for so much . . . for the rare and rewarding opportunity of knowing a wild, endearing family of black eagles and for being part of our film *For the Love of an Eagle* with Arthur and Peter . . . for the warmth and unflagging interest of my splendid family, who shared my joy and my heartache, in so many ways . . . for the delightful enthusiasm of my friends, always eager to listen to my eagle adventures . . . for the friendship of that grand literary man, G. H. Calpin, my stern critic, without whose steadfast encouragement this book would not have been completed.

I would like to record my sincerest appreciation for the willing and helpful cooperation of the South African Department of Information, which so readily agreed to the reproduction of some of the frames from our film *For the Love of an Eagle,* made on their behalf by Arthur Bowland and myself. And to the National Geographic Society of Washington, D.C., which so generously provided copies of my pictures from my story published in their magazine and for which they hold the copyright.

Contents

Prologue: Mated Until Death

So the struck eagle stretch'd upon the plain,
No more through rolling clouds to soar again.
                    BYRON

The sound of the shot froze lizards and hyraxes into gargoyles of terror; and the sudden stillness was so intense that the gale itself seemed to stay in its onslaught. In the late afternoon rain threatened in the ragged clouds as the sun pulled the day over the high towers of the Drakensberg Mountains toward the endless ranges of Lesotho.

Only one thing moved. A black eagle began to fall from the sky, the spread of its great wings crumpling in grotesque outline. High above, pinned against the void, now alone and suddenly incomplete, its mate watched the crazy plummeting course earthward. A desolate cry tore from it, and the gale caught at the sound, sending it echoing through ravines and crevices until, in rising crescendo, it rang as a challenge to the mountain world. And, with the cry, the crier, too, dropped.

The great living body planed down with controlled purpose across the mountain's face. Then abruptly, as though conscious for the first time of danger, it winged over and sped once again to the clouds.

There it hung, bewildered, as it quartered each segment of its

1

domain with its fantastic sight. Its gaze came back always to its fallen mate, a black smudge on the mountainside.

The earth was splashed with the colors of autumn. Families of hyraxes squirmed in the lingering warmth of the rocks. A band of vultures, golden-bellied in the setting sun, winged over aimlessly, indifferent to the eagle's cry.

Nothing escaped the searching eyes of the eagle. As sun glinted on metal, it watched the gunman moving among the boulders. The outline of him was imprinted on its being, the distinctive form of something to be avoided, hated.

Half in anger, half in need of confirmation, it turned from him, circled, and dropped height, alighting on a slab of rock jutting over its mate. It cawed distractedly as it jumped down and stumped over the rough ground where it stood looking at the mass of black plumes and the giant wing, white-tipped, flung in wide, unconscious grace. Blood flowed from the neck and the white of the back was stained with red.

A gust of wind stirred the inanimate feathers and the living eagle leaned forward excitedly and thrust its beak against the sprawling body. There was no answer to the beguiling sounds it made, none to the motions of eagle tenderness. With neck and chest close to the ground, it nudged the unmoving body, imploring acknowledgment. There was no response.

Suddenly its pleading ceased. A hiss of impatience tinged with fear escaped it, as it sought to stir reply to its cries. Then the hiss changed to peremptory sounds of exasperation, as though to force the body back to life. Uncomprehending, it crouched down protectively near, wanting to give comfort, seeking comfort for itself.

For a time it could not accept the knowledge that flooded its being, that not again would these magnificent wings span the world they had shared for so long. The regal eyes were lifeless, and it moved away, knowing, swinging into an updraught toward the darkening sky.

Suddenly, another shot splintered the mountain world.

The rising eagle shuddered and floundered, fighting to keep aloft and shaking its great body as if to rid it of shock.

Far below, a man cursed, angry that he had missed an easy shot, half hoping he had not, seeing the eagle grope for height as it struggled beyond his vision. He had got one of them, anyway, he consoled himself, as he made his way down the mountain.

The eagle, unable to go naturally into the wind, flapped madly to keep some semblance of balance, and made automatically in the direction of the aerie. Its right leg trailed; pain daggered as it tried to stretch it up into its customary position beneath its tail. It drifted uncertainly, incapable of immediate decision until, once again, the momentary flash of the sun on a gun exploded across its tired eyes. Intuitively it banked as it caught a glimpse of the man, then steadied itself, drawn to the sight.

The giant bird was consumed with atavistic fury. Its great body surged with it. Man had never come into its focus of attack before and it hung a moment, confused by the overwhelming impulse to translate anger into violence. It lunged down in a deadly stoop, knowing instinctively that it lacked the clean, fluid movement for a good strike, but feeling viciously satisfied.

The man was aware of a powerful rush of wind around him and yelled as he sprang for the protection of the rocks. Then silence enveloped him and he looked up, shaken. "Must have been imagining things," he muttered. The sky was empty.

Its moment spent, the eagle labored past known buttresses, familiarly steering its course until, caught up in a rising wind, it spiraled towards a cluster of pine trees thrusting up from a river bed, hundreds of feet below. It thrashed against the higher branches, and found a foothold with the talons of its sound leg and sank down, its proud head drooped in draining defeat.

The bird knew no comfort. Its call was a female's longing for her mate, a special voice tuned of request and demand that the male so seldom denies. Full of ardent need of him she croaked her grief to the mountains, yet knowing in the strange way understood only to the wild that her mate would never soar with her again. Her first love, the love to whom she was pledged, as humans are pledged, "until death do us part."

The echo of the shots reverberated in the foothills. Farmers, riding home from outlying fields, squinted upward, wondering at their target. African farmhands saw an eagle fall, heard the sound of a yell after the second shot, and shook their heads in grave superstition. They waited for the mate to fall and, when they did not see it, looked at each other and breathed "Hau!", knowing it had fled to the dwelling place of their own ancestral spirits, up there in the heaven country, and that one day it would return to look for its mate. Yes, they nodded, one day that messenger of the gods would return to look for its mate.

Not so many years ago eagles nested away from the main range of Natal's Drakensberg. They found solitary mountains or outcrop ridges and spurs and were reasonably safe. Man had not yet pushed roads through to the mountains. But, as he began to intrude more and more, the aerial giants made for the inaccessible peaks. Only those pairs with nesting sites as yet unthreatened returned each year, clinging to their homes. Some of the farms hugging the Drakensberg, tracts of land that have been in the same families for generations, look upon these black eagles as "our eagles," as part of their heritage.

These two were a familiar sight. Men knew them almost as their own, and often looked up, reining in their horses to watch them painting their beauty in breathtaking strokes across the sky.

"Look," they would say, "the eagles have come back to nest. Autumn must be here."

The eagles' return meant the coming of cold. They came to hatch out their young when the snow lay about the mountains, at the beginning of July, here below Capricorn. And, if some of the farmers wondered if the winged predators helped themselves to a few of their newborn lambs, they still found it hard to press a trigger when an eagle's giant shadow rippled over their acres.

The man with the gun was a newcomer. He was nonplussed when he boasted of his success and saw the looks of disapproval in the farmers' eyes. They looked up. No eagles spanned the sky.

The gunman must have shot both eagles, they decided.

> *The wind blows out of the gates of the day*
> *The wind blows over the lonely of heart,*
> *And the lonely of heart is withered away . . .*
>   YEATS

But the female eagle lived! At first light she stirred. The sky was marbled in pastels of blue and pink, and there was a stillness that only a mountain dawn can give. The cold had stiffened her leg, and

4

she winced as she moved. She saw the sky reflected in a pool of rainwater trapped in a boulder. Undaunted by height and distance as she was, the short flight from the tree to the mountainside now seemed quite beyond her will.

As the dawn's glow spread, she felt an urgency to be gone. She dropped from the branch, opened her wings and floated down across the precipice to the boulder. She fell against it, and for a while lay there as though indifferent to her fate.

But the great eagle heart of hers dragged her body up and she drank thirstily of the water.

The mist on the horizon began to clear as the sun changed the pine trees into torches of flame, and the eagle drank again, filling her being with the ice-cold liquid. She stood for a moment picking at the dried blood on her leg, then lumbered down the slope in pathetic awkwardness over the rough ground until she came to the edge of the escarpment. As she became clumsily airborne there was no joy in her wings, only a tenacious perseverance that forced her up out of sight beyond the clouds. She looked toward her mountain home, then started on the long glide away to the mighty refuge of the inaccessible ranges, grieving for her mate.

> . . . *So she arose from her home in the hills and down through*
> *the blossoms that danced with their shadows*
> *Out of the blue of the dreaming distance, down to the heart of her*
> *lover she came . . .*
>
> NOYES

It was a long time before her hunting was filled with the old zest and cunning, a long time before her body, starved during the time her torn leg prevented her from finding food, filled out and became hard again. She kept to the remote central ranges. Sight of humans, though seldom encountered, prompted an alien instinct of defiance. She flew great distances, seldom going near the mountain of horror. Even the sight of a pair of eagles starting on their nest did little to stir her.

Then, suddenly, everything changed!

One day, dropping to a lofty pinnacle, she became aware of a young male quietly watching her.

She stared back at him and, without warning, burst with elemental longing. The need for a mate surged through her. He was very much younger than she, but she had no time for search or choice. And, once she had set her mind and heart on him, he would be won by the sheer power of her love. He, knowing little of the look of a wooing female, was oblivious of his destiny.

A reckless urgency possessed her. Memory returned to the spur, and the aerie on the rock ledge, abandoned this long time, was now vitally important to her. That was her territory, her home, and she would return to it with a mate.

At first her attention meant nothing to the young male. He had seen others of his kind, but this female was something beyond his experience. He tried to dismiss her and unconcernedly roused his feathers as she took off in a spiral and swooped past him, demanding acknowledgment. When he ignored her, she alighted beside him, leaned over and pecked him in labored fun. He shied away, hissing, and arched his neck in protest. Not in the slightest put off, she looked at him intently, then tried again.

As an eaglet of eight months, he had been chased from his birthplace by his parents, his life with them over as soon as he was able to fend for himself. Since then he had lived a lonely life and the first year taught him that the ease with which his parents had always seemed to produce food was a lesson that had to be learned. It was not built-in. Often he was very hungry.

Now, just over four years old, he was a mature black eagle. Each year's molt had produced progressively blacker plumage but little other change. In his prime, sap rising, he had yet no awareness of his status as a potential mate, or warning of the pools of purpose shining in this large female's eyes. But something of her communicated to him. He found that when she flew away from him, he waited for her return; and that when she reappeared, he was glad yet nervous of her nearness as she hopped over to him.

The intricate pattern of her flying pleasurably drained him of the will to protest. The warm sun filled him with languor. But, even in this placid contentment, he still held back encouragement.

Eventually, when she appeared to tire of him and flashed down a ravine beyond him, he was conscious of a different sensation. His erstwhile lonely world, now so overpoweringly filled with company, was empty again, and it was past enduring. His loneliness was intensified. When he could bear it no longer he rose quickly and followed her into the vast unknown, reluctant, but powerless to resist. And somehow he knew, with innate fatalism, that he belonged with her.

> *Why having won her do I woo*
> *Because her spirit's vestal grace*
> *Provokes me always to pursue*
> *But spiritlike eludes embrace . . .*
>
> PATMORE

He sulked. The giant bird, all female, had enticed him away from the safety of the peaks to this dubious place with every sign of humans. There was no denying her magnetism. Each time she left him, he was desolate.

She knew this mountain and the spread of the land. Her superiority disgruntled him. He chased her, angry. She seemed to delight in escaping him. He was confused at what she wanted, so he stood watching her on the ledge with the mound of moldy old sticks that greatly excited her. He understood none of it. When she called eagerly to him, he ignored her, yet still was drawn to her. Impatiently, she turned from him, rose in the air, and missed his first tentative male move toward her.

Disappointed, he brooded as he followed her flight and shouted as she rushed past him, lashing out her talons. Something all male enveloped him at this naked display of purpose, and he longed to answer in like manner. But he felt keenly her dismissal of him as she rolled in the sky.

Furious, he pounded his feet as she spiraled out of sight. Then she was back, tantalizing him as she dropped down and briefly pecked him before racing away again. His wings twitched and something of her wild exhilaration called to him. He stood quite still, stunned by the sudden knowledge that her aerial display was staged for him alone. His senses rippled with excitement. He lifted his head to her in admiration and tenderness, trembling with gladness.

At last the earth could hold him no longer. He swept into the freshening wind, called to her.

The female felt the strong call. Her web was spun. She had only to wait. So she gave herself up to the freedom of the sky.

7

The wind caught him up and the female planed down, touching his body as she passed. He shivered and followed, ringing up after her until the earth was a haze. He lost sight of her and was jubilant, quite sure he had outstripped her, but she was suddenly at his side and they wheeled together before he had time to feel rancor.

He seemed unable to handle the enormity of what was happening to him. The vigor of his flying, perfected over the years, lacked the heady force of hers and he felt clumsy compared to her. But, as his eyes followed her wings beating at the sky, he acknowledged her dominant strength, and gradually became less daunted by it. Every fiber of his being told him that he wanted to be her protector, her companion, the defender of her realm. He turned from her, feeling the necessity to fly alone before irrevocably committing himself.

The cold wind cut. Quickened with energy, power coiled in him like a flame. Exploding in wild happiness, he raced after her and suddenly she banked in alarm as he hurtled down on her. Her acknowledgment spurred him on to force her to his flying will. This was his mate. He soared, ablaze with discovery. And she, too, knew that he was her love.

The long halcyon days of courting began and their mating flights traced their love across the sky. The union of black eagles is a deep, psychological affair—strong and longer than that of most species of the wild. Their rapt tenderness drew them closer until their flight seemed incomplete, one without the other. Each tried to outdo the other in majestic and intricate display. They mated often, but sometimes it was almost incidental to the exhilaration of the flight that prompted it. They were mated until death parted them, knowing that to find joy in each other, knowing each other and relying on each other, was to survive.

Trusty, dusky, vivid, true,
With eyes of gold and bramble-dew,
Steel true and blade-straight,
The great artificer made my mate . . .
STEVENSON

Their honeymoon began at the end of March. The male was tireless, filled with enthusiasm.

He, being smaller, had greater maneuverability than his mate, but her wider wingspan gave her more capacity for speed and height. The sky spun with their wild beauty as their wings lofted them into the wind away from the earth. When they returned it was in a series of loops, sweeping toward each other, locking talons and beaks, to roll downward until, wings and tails braking, they flashed free and launched their quivering bodies in separate drives upward again.

The male explored his new territory and soon knew it as she did. They hunted together, he learning from her to know things that were man-dangerous, food that was too easy, too suspiciously a handout. While food was plentiful they hunted alone, but when their staple diet of hyraxes became scarce, they turned to guinea fowl or partridge and this required dual hunting. If they had to turn to larger prey, such as buck or baboons, this, too, would require their combined effort.

At first the male was inexpert, uncertain of what was required of him. But his mate showed him that he could implicitly depend on her and that she, in turn, trusted him absolutely. Under the aura of her approval, he learned fast.

Nevertheless, the first time he was successful, it took him by surprise. He was gliding lazily when he became aware of his mate's absorption in the ground immediately beneath them. He joined her, but noticed nothing unusual—grass, stunted bushes in abundance, but no rocks beloved by hyraxes. Bored, he veered off to look for more hopeful hunting grounds, but at her call they continued to float and circle, losing height, and he saw that the shadows under the bushes were no longer still. There was a tremor of movement, imperceptible as the ripples of a pebble on a limpid pool, out of place in the windless day.

Patiently she waited, certain that it would not be she who made the first move. He was not quite sure what would happen, but followed close behind. The purple patch was coming to life. It disintegrated into a dozen fragments as guinea fowl scattered away from the menacing shadows above them. Most of them made for the thin protection of other bushes; but one, frenzied into fatal error, ran wildly along in the open grass.

9

The female eagle closed her wings and shot down, talons thrust forward. A series of loops and glides closed the distance. She called quickly to her mate and he followed with instinctive realization of what he had to do. Their prey was swerving and weaving. The female knew that a running target was difficult to pin down. She slid toward it, taking her time and, not satisfied, leveled out her flight and cut back again, this time coming down at a sharper angle until she was just above it. She was not concerned with the perfect aim required for snatching hyraxes from hard rocks, for here the earth was soft turf and would not harm her talons. And this time she was only part of the plan.

She gathered her forces and dropped in a running dive at the fleeing guinea fowl and struck it with her body and tail. The impact sent it flying as she continued the arc of her flight. Behind her the male swept in, wrapped his talons round the stunned prey, then followed his mate to the summit of the mountain.

They slept on the same buttress each night, wings touching, nuzzling each other in deep contentment, waking with the dawn to another day of close companionship. He wanted no other life.

Then, one morning, he sensed the beginning of change in her. Gone were the soft loving gestures she had showered on him. Ferocity marked her flight. She became impatient when he was playful. He dived down at her, expecting their usual rapport. She flashed out with her beak and razed his back. He retaliated, angry, and matched her talon for talon as they executed a series of hard, feet-locked loops and savage spirals, corkscrewing down to the escarpment where he dropped next to her, hesitant until he saw her crouching, her eyes on him—she consumed with the deep demand within her to get ready for the laying of her eggs.

The honeymoon was over.

> *Let us then be up and doing*
> *With a heart for any fate,*
> *Still achieving, still pursuing,*
> *Learn to labor and to wait . . .*
> LONGFELLOW

She was a formidable homemaker. He fetched and carried for her. Although she did her share, he sensed that hers was a labor of love. He was cowed when she found fault with everything he did, and was intrigued by the ungainly pile of sticks and branches as it grew higher. For all its untidiness, it was strongly and compactly made, securely based on the ledge. It would be able to withstand the harsh elements to which, except for a slight overhang, it was exposed. The aerie they made was about three feet high and a ragged five feet wide.

Often he was chagrined at her ability to break off large dead branches as she jumped up and down on them, and then, as they started to fall, swoop to retrieve them with her talons before they hit the ground. Once at the aerie, she dropped a branch and positioned it with her beak, moving it until she was satisfied that it fitted where she wanted it. If he proudly planed in with something she thought did not measure up to her building plans, she promptly heaved it over the side.

When the nest was nearly completed, he sought again the sweet companionship of their first days but she turned on him, impatient to finish building. Soon all it required was the soft central basin that would hold the eggs.

When the driving tension lessened, she called to him with her former gentleness, wanting him to share her anticipation. He responded eagerly and when, next morning, they went in search of the leafy twigs that would line the basin, he was proud that he was part of the mysterious happenings involving the aerie, satisfied that she needed him.

In the early mist they rose from the ledge. She flew with him in all their previous rapture, and their mating flight was witnessed only by the sun-bursting clouds, the wind and the mountain turrets. They vied with each other as they lunged up side by side and he shared the forceful lovemaking with pounding zest.

The first egg was laid at the beginning of June. They slept on the ledge beside the aerie, awakening to each other's throaty whispering. Often she stretched over and probed his neck feathers gently with her beak, and he cawed softly in response. Despite his love, he was all custodian of this rock ledge that now held his family. When dawn broke, he knew that the days of hunting for two were about to begin.

On the following day, the second egg was laid. This was more rounded than the other, and was plain off-white compared to the first one's red-brown blotches. The female settled firmly down over them, the feathers down her breastbone parting to allow the warmth of her body to touch them. By starting to brood them at the same time, there would not be two days' difference in their hatching.

She had a long wait—between forty-one and forty-four days. Then the eggs, in their own way, would let her know that the vigil was over. The shells would grow progressively thinner, the membrane inside softer, so that the tiny serrations on the eaglets' beaks could tear their way from the security of the egg through membrane and shell. That done, the saw would disappear.

The male became restless, especially as he found it necessary to hunt only every few days since the female ate less than usual. He would circle their territory and keep an eye on the buzzards on the far side of the mountain, but hour after hour he stood motionless on the escarpment above her.

He felt shut out by her absorption. He was devoted to her and became increasingly anxious that she should have some respite from being on the nest day after day, facing gales, rain and snow.

Only rarely did she respond to his persistent offers of help, then she acquiesced suddenly. Raising herself from the eggs, she stood for a moment, took off, and immediately spiraled to the heights. The first time the male tried to follow she chased him back, making it plain that the only reason she agreed to his persuasion was because he would be at home to guard the eggs.

He looked into the basin, puzzled at its contents that took up all his mate's attention and time. He hoped they would be worth the waiting. He moved over carefully and, after one or two nervous attempts, lowered himself on the eggs. As he settled over them, he watched the female brace herself against the gale. His being soared with her, his wings twitched in longing to be there with her. But when she returned, he was almost sorry.

She waited. And, as she sat, she watched this young mate of hers, her hooded eyes filled with pride as she followed his fast-improving feats in the sky. The shadow of the past still held its remembered terrors and always would, but they began to pale a little against the splendid reality of the young eagle she had claimed as her own.

She had hatched out other chicks during her long life. Every one had had her passionate, undivided love and care while it was dependent on her. Each time, in the brooding, she felt a profound peace, a stirring of some other world beneath her that was part of her. And, when the eggs could no longer confine the demanding life within, she never failed to feel the same soaring rush of joy at the sound of the first, triumphant "cheep. . . ."

A Bell and Beginnings

. . . The lines are fallen unto me in pleasant
places; yea, I have a goodly heritage . . .
PSALMS

Someone once asked me, "How can you possibly enjoy the constant battle against the elements, returning to the mountains again and again just to be with wild predators that are not likely to show you much friendship?"

How to reply but to wish you could see an eagle standing on a crag with the clouds behind it, or spread out against the sky's blue in lines of simple greatness, the emblem of courage since time began.

An eagle is heraldic and has a firm place in legend. And it always gives me a good feeling that the birth of a nation like America is so symbolically tied up with the beauty and strength of an eagle, its wings spreading protectively, wisely, and with great grace over all its people. Here in South Africa they are still miraculously alive, but for how long, who can tell? To know them is a rewarding experience. Despite their fierce strength, eagles are tender and devoted to each other. An eaglet is cuddly and endearing. Youngsters of any species are always cute, and a baby predator, woolly and friendly, is no exception.

But I could not really miss loving mountains and their giant birds with the ancestors and parents I have.

It is, to me, an inevitable and happy thought that eagles and the story of my love for them should have its beginning in the Drakensberg Mountains, safe as a surrounding wall, that guard Natal, the province of my birth, and give sanctuary to many of the big birds so fast becoming extinct. Both giant predators and the mighty range are compellingly beautiful, both are molded in majestic proportions; and mountains and the birds that fly above them are a splendid blend of the wild. They were always there, birds of prey in cloud-touching loveliness, but as distant as the sky in which they flew. Until one day I climbed The Bell, a 9,757-foot peak in the Drakensberg, and came face to face with a pair of black eagles.

As do most people born in Natal, I regard the "Berg" as my personal heritage. The great "Mountains of the Dragon" curl in ancient silence round "The Garden Province," which rolls from them one hundred miles, as the migrant swallow flies, to the Indian Ocean. A recumbent monster with stone ribs curved out in colossal ridges from scaly heights, it has notches on its vertebrae that stand out in clear peaks along the three hundred miles of its gargantuan spine.

It sprawls as the natural border between South Africa and Lesotho, the latter being all that remains of the vast basalt cap that once covered the whole of the Southern African plateau. Lesotho stretches westward from the Dragon's back, the monstrous side heaving, fold upon fold, treeless, snow-capped, seemingly to infinity. It lifts a prehistoric head to 10,470 feet in the shape of Sentinel Peak and, from there, ripples its coarse skin into fantastic shapes and outlines, wrinkles its body into wondrous ramparts, humps its back into pinnacles and fluted valleys, on into the lower hills of the tail . . . a monster beloved with pride.

Apart from a deep love of this mountain world, my family has a special historical interest in it. The courageous journeys of South Africa's pioneers into the unknown abound with romance and adventure. In Natal we are conscious, always, of what those first intrepid settlers must have felt when, after hazardous months of traveling, they arrived at the edge of the awesome 10,000-foot drop into Natal, and had to negotiate cumbersome wagons down ravines and gorges to reach the promised land below.

One of the country's best known pioneers was my mother's

great-grandfather, the Reverend James Archbell, who came from Yorkshire in 1818 to be a missionary amongst the Baralong tribe in Bechuana Country (the Transvaal of today). Known as "the master trekker," he had penetrated the uninhabited wilds of South Africa ten years before the first Voortrekker left the Cape. He and his wife, Elizabeth, were the first pioneers to set eyes on the future Witwatersrand, the first to publish a book—a reader for the Tswana people.

This great-great-grandfather of mine had a casual disregard for the dangers to be faced in reaching faraway places. "The distance of Natal from Graham's Town is by land something more than 500 miles. A 17 days' ride," he wrote, "averaging at least 35 miles per diem, brought me to the Dutch camp on the Umlazi, eight miles from the Port [Durban]. On my arrival they received me cordially and assembled from all the adjacent parts to attend Divine Worship . . ." After completing his mission—to report on the happenings in as yet unnamed Durban—he mounted his horse and rode back to Grahamstown.

As children, one of the stories of our ancestors we liked best was the carrying off, by the Matabele tribe, of little Joseph, the missionary's son. They demanded a ransom of white oxen. The near impossibility of laying hands on a span of these did not daunt the boy's father.

Some twenty months after his son had been kidnapped, and after unbelievable adventures, little Joseph was back with his family, the debt to the Matabele paid in full.

My great-great-grandfather wrote with pride and everlasting wonder of his new country, and I cannot help but think of him each time I see the lovely land spread out before me, as he must have seen it when he wrote in September of 1841: ". . . each part rising in beauty and rich fertility above the other as we proceed eastward, the verdant hills and prolific valleys, fertilised by inexhaustible streams, teeming with rich vegetation of great variety . . . fully justify the rapturous exclamations and glowing imagery employed in their description. The view of the country from a high eminence is enchantingly picturesque and romantic . . ."

He was known to Afrikaners and Zulus as "Aartspiel," a phonetic translation of Archbell, and two Boer leaders, particularly, found in him a kindred spirit. Potgieter, unable to persuade Dutch Reformed churchmen to accompany him over "the formidable barrier," asked the Reverend Archbell to be his official chaplain. And Piet Retief, famous leader of the Great Trek from the Cape, wrote, "Who could be better found, better equipped to live at peace with Voortrekker and Zulu alike than James Archbell. He deserves the highest praise . . . and it is to be wished that all those people who profess to teach and lead the uncivilised would take a lesson from him and conduct them in the same paths of religion, industry and justice. . . ."

My father was a Scot who had come to South Africa as a very young man to seek his fortune, and he was fond of saying that he had found it when he married my mother. Having left the golden eagles and stags he had known in the Highlands, he happily adopted the mountains of Natal and the wild they had to offer.

We lived nine miles from Durban on fourteen acres of land. My brother, sisters and I knew every bird in a countryside abounding with undisturbed creatures of the wild.

To my parents the flora and fauna of God's good earth were things to be loved and protected, and we were aware that, as humans, the supposed superior beings, we had a responsibility to the lesser beings and that their destiny was in the hands of man. We spent a great deal of our holiday time in the Drakensberg, to which we were introduced at a very early age, and here we delighted in the discovery of a whole new range of birds and animals. Never did two people love their life more than my parents. In the latter years of their lives they lived at Umhlanga Rocks, at that time a tiny village on the north coast which, until a national route cut through, was about fifteen miles from Durban and reached only by a rough, circuitous road. Their constan delight was the small indigenous forest and the "river of reeds," which in Zulu is known as *Umhlanga*. With that charm brought from bygone days, I seldom heard my father call my mother by her Christian name, although everyone else, including her grandchildren, called her "Ida." But how often I heard him exclaim, "If heaven is as bonny as Umhlanga Rocks and the Drakensberg, Mrs. Cowden, it must be a gae braw place."

In the mountains, watching the giants in the sky the Zulus believe is heaven, I think of these things and of their rich heritage. Sometimes I wonder if the eagles flying across my skies are the great-great-offspring of those an ancestral missionary saw. It is possible, and I like to think they are.

> *Abrupt with eagle speed she cut the sky*
> *Instant invisible to mortal eye:*
> *Then first he recognized the ethereal guest . . .*
>
> POPE

The Bell stands aloof, a mountain of solid rock alone and absolute as though it exploded into being, thrusting up from the center of the earth in fiery impatience, and leaving all around it a chaos of gigantic debris as it shrugged away from the neighboring peaks of an impressive range. When the mist curls round it, it seems to hang from a mighty, invisible hand, waiting only for divine sign to boom from the belfry of the heavens its deep call to believers.

I was once persuaded to accompany two mountaineers in their attempt to negotiate the Bell. Since I was not conversant with mountain climbs that required roping up, always having found ropes irksome and preferring to go where my own two feet can take me, I accepted that the normal route was across the outer face. I agreed to accompany the climbers only because it was their last day before returning to Cape Town, and they dearly wanted to add the Bell to their other mountaineering achievements.

Wind blew straight off the snow as we inched up the cold and deadly mountain face, and I was convinced I was the first person ever to climb without toes and fingers! I listened to the wind and the voices of my companions above it, and surveyed the summits serried round me. When, in the late afternoon, we reached the top of the Bell, Lesotho spread before us, a blanket tossed onto the map of South Africa.

All round the land-locked little kingdom of Lesotho the map is crisscrossed with every evidence of progress and people in a hurry: highways, railways and blacked-in cities. But the cartographical legend of Lesotho is wondrously devoid of the broad bands depicting major communication networks and large dots denoting cities. Instead, there are uninhabited mountain ranges and sources of great rivers, blatant space and people not herded together in great enough numbers to qualify for a dot. Most of it is so inaccessible that the only way to travel is on horse or foot. The country is poor in almost everything except the gems of its scenery and the wealth of big birds in its skies.

Moshoeshoe, the founder of Lesotho, whose grandfather Peete had been eaten by cannibals during the journey to the new and awesome country in the mountains, could neither read nor write, yet he became a statesman and founded a nation from scattered, primitive and warring tribes that he was pleased to say was "safely folded in the arms of my Queen"—Queen Victoria, whom he greatly revered. He had his scribe write to her, "My country is like a blanket, O my Queen ..." And that is how Lesotho looked from the top of the Bell, a country royally purple, mantled with ermine snows.

I watched as Tom, one of my climbing partners, disappeared over the edge of the first downward pitch. "You are next," said James. I spread out my hands, and he exploded, "You just cannot be serious!" I had never abseiled in my life.

There is a first time for everything. Clinging to the slender strands that kept my body from the rocks far below, I had the wild feeling that if my feet, feeling their way down the rock face, kicked out, the Bell would begin to peal forth. A light snow began to fall.

It was July 18, midwinter, the grass brown and dry in the crevices. A novice, I listened to the discussion about the difficulties of securing a piton, and wondered at the recurrence of the word *wongs*. I thought it a strange mountaineering term—a sort of gremlin or polperro-pisky of the peaks—until I discovered, much later, that we doubtless owed our lives to Mr. and Mrs. Wongtschowski, the only other two people at the time who had climbed the Bell up and down the front face where we now squatted. A piton driven in by them on their epic climb was still there, corroded but hopeful. And I hunched on the ledge, watching in odd disbelief as each tug of the rope from the abseiling mountaineers sagged the piton.

The last of the sun illuminated the back of Cathedral Peak, and long shadows began to cover the mountains in the decorous habits of monks. I ran my hands over the ravaged rock where I waited and they came away dripping, icy. High above, vultures watched the flashes of movement on the Bell, waiting for a last-minute meal. Mist hung all about, a laurel wreath on the mountain's shoulders and, all around me, the peaks reared out of the foaming white ...

still . . . immense. A strange peace that overwhelmed fear reached out, and I did not glance at the near-horizontal piton since it seemed no longer the pivot on which my life hung. If this is to be my moment in time, I thought, maybe the Bell will throb with music.

But it was not music that the Bell gave me. On a wave in the mist in lazy orbit floated a black eagle. We looked at each other, eyes level, almost within touching distance, astonished at our meeting. Then, with a casual flip-over of its wing it was gone, leaving its jet-black outline seared on my snow-tired eyes. Again it glided round. This time it tilted up over me as it passed and the whole spread of its lovely wings and the light "windows" formed by the tips of the long primary feathers let in the gold of the sinking sun, seeming to draw me up with it. The eagle peered at me, unbelieving, not even afraid. And how marvelously alive it looked in the cold enormity round me. The next time it returned it brought its mate with it as if to corroborate an unlikely story.

The eagles continued their circling, but when, at last, they became bored with the insignificant human crouching on the mountain, and sped off into a mist-filled gorge below me, I could not move, could not break the spell they had spun around the Bell. Nor have I ever. Such moments occur seldom, and this one I would never forget. There was nothing in my mind but the thought of the birds of the mist.

They had assumed splendid face. I would look up, now, and they would have identity. I knew them, had been close to them, and would go looking for that nearness again.

The searching was often lonely. I found many eagles but they were deep in the heart of the mountains. Once, in a light aircraft between Himeville and Mokhotlong, the administrative capital of Lesotho, where I had gone to search for them, a lammergeyer kept pace with us and the shadows of bird and plane rippled together over the timeless land beneath us. I traveled by foot, on horseback, by Land Rover.

Once, too, I spent ten snowbound days at the top of Sani Pass, my only company a handful of Basotho and the giant predators in the sky. This pass, once used exclusively by horse-trains to bring the wool from Lesotho down into Natal and take grain back, links Lesotho to Natal in a dramatic way. Nine miles of zigzags, it has a gradient often one in five, and the last four miles rise 4,000 feet to the rim, 9,400 feet above sea level. The only movement in the vast wastes of white, frozen to immobility, was that of the birds wheeling above. When I rode the gleaming wonderland on skis, their shadows raced with me.

Here I found three more black eagles. Along the crenellating escarpment, enormous ravines cut back into the massif, and the comparatively warmer air from Natal melted the overhang of snow, leaving for a few yards back a narrow ribbon of sodden turf. I rode a sturdy mountain pony or walked, accompanied by a small Basotho boy, one afternoon coming across a pair of black eagles tugging at a dead sheep.

A host of vultures domed the sky. A group of wild horses thundered by. Suddenly a third black eagle, much larger than the other two, swooped in, sending the vultures off in alarm and a flurry of feathers. Like the "three black and midnight hags" of Macbeth, the predators hissed, arched necks, clicked beaks and furiously flapped their wings. But the lone attacker was the clear winner and it ate greedily. Eventually, replete, it dropped off the edge of the escarpment and glided arrogantly and heavily down into Natal.

The people in the huts offered a great deal of information and gave many directions, but I was never quite sure where fact ended and legend began, whether the eagles they knew were real ones or those so closely tied up with their belief that the spirits of their ancestors live up in the heaven country beyond the clouds. They listened to the boy as he told them wide-eyed of the large eagle. They nodded. This one they knew. This one was, indeed, a living legend.

From the escarpment the flanks of Natal's foothills lay like the thick ruffles of a velvet green curtain. Razor-edged ridges and long valleys of waving grass eased the land from the heights to the undulating hills. If I were an eagle, I thought, I would never venture away from this splendid land. I was gathering my own personal harvest of eagles but, when I looked down at the one fast disappearing, I wondered if I should not, after all, be content to be with birds in the more accessible hills far below. Then I looked up and saw that the pair of eagles hung in the sky watching me, and I knew I could not give them up.

The lone eagle sailed indolently down into Natal; effortlessly steered its course through ravines, over outcrops; curved its wings past buttresses. And as I watched, without knowing it, included in the vast panorama before me and where the eagle flew was a spur of the Drakensberg that was to hold me in its thrall in the years to come.

Plunderers of the Sky

*When thou seest an eagle, thou seest a
portion of Genius; lift up thy head.*
WILLIAM BLAKE

South Africa's black eagle is a true eagle.

Of all the birds of prey that form the order Falconiformes—well over two hundred fifty species, including eagles, falcons, buzzards, vultures, harriers, hawks and kestrels—a true eagle is the only one with its legs feather-covered down to its toes. The others have scaly, bare legs from the "knee" down.

The word *predator* means "one that lives by preying on others; seeks prey; lives by plundering." Each species has its own way of seeking and eating its prey. A vulture is not equipped as a killer; it feeds on dead meat. An eagle, though not averse to carrion, prefers to hunt live food. The dainty pygmy falcon, about the size of a swallow, is a ruthless little killer that tackles prey much larger than itself—usually other birds. It has greater claim to the title of predator than the lammergeyer, which is a hundred times larger but does not kill its food.

A bird of prey flies to live. Its wings, the most vital part of its makeup, are specialized tools of flight that help it to find food and kill its find. A vulture's large, broad wings are not fashioned for speed. It has no need to take food that is already dead by surprise.

It is so heavy that the constant flapping, necessary with smaller wings, would be extremely energy-consuming. It floats high in the sky, away from danger, and goes many hundreds of miles looking for an animal stationary enough to indicate death. Then it glides down, its wings taut, and, without a flap, judges the distance so that it lands within a few yards of its meal.

Birds that hunt live food have wings less sail-like than the vulture. A falcon chases its prey; its long, narrow wings give it great speed and the capacity for quick change in direction. Although it can soar, it is light and cannot do so for long. It flies above its victim and "stoops in" with the lightning speed the structure of its wings allows, following the twists and turns of the doomed bird with devastating accuracy.

The kestrel's wings, broader than the falcon's, make it a master in the art of hovering. Its main diet is lizards, rats and snakes, creatures difficult to see from above in the grassy, open fields where they live. The kestrel spreads its wings against the wind, moving them constantly, fanning its tail to keep its height and position, watching for movement below that will prompt a downward plunge.

The tail of a predator acts as a rudder. Its ten or twelve strong feathers open and close like a fan. The hunters have powerful tails so that they can brake against the tremendous draught created as they plunge. They can "stand on the wind" as they start on the upward flight; as they soar, the tail moves all the time, fanning the wind, steering the bird's course.

A vulture, on the other hand, has a weak tail. It does not dive at great speed. Predators that live mainly in forests have short, broad wings to allow them to fly easily among the tree trunks. Speed in searching for food in undergrowth is not as important as being able to turn quickly and drop down suddenly, both actions perfected by a longer tail.

The beaks and feet of predators are also specialized weapons. Except in a few instances, a predator's beak is not used to catch food; nor, with the upper mandible curving over the lower, is it designed to peck. It is made to rip and tear, hook and wrench. The falcon is one of the few that kills with its beak. It does so on the wing. The upper section of its beak has a sawlike part in the middle with which to cut the flesh and crunch the bones of its small prey without the need to tear it to bits.

A large vulture's beak is capacious and strong. Usually one of the earliest of the scavengers to appear on the scene of a dead animal, it is allowed the dubious honor of getting at the meat first, ripping at the sinew and muscle, dismembering the carcass and swallowing enormous portions. One of the smallest vultures has a long, thin, probelike beak, used to reach delicately into cavities to pick at the meat too difficult for larger beaks to manage.

A bird of prey's natural element is the air. It is not comfortable on the ground, the natural function of its feet being to kill, carry and help in the eating process, rather than to hop or walk. Normally, one toe points backward, three forward. A victim has little hope of escape if the pincher grip is thrust at a vulnerable spot. An eagle breaks its quarry's neck with a quick flick of these two lethal talons.

The falcon, besides its special beak, has a middle toe longer than normal. This allows it extended reach to grasp and bind its fast-flying prey. A vulture has little need of specially developed toes, except for a "longer forefinger" with which to anchor itself against the carrion while its beak tugs at the food. Eagles and ospreys that live on fish have feet to enable them to catch a slippery victim. Their toes are balanced to give a firm, steady grasp—two forward and two backward. Underneath their feet are rasplike ridges which make holding a wet, squirming body a great deal easier. A predator's feet are bare, so that dirt and mess from the things it eats can quickly and easily be cleaned off. An exception is the owl, which belongs to the order Strigiformes. It has feathers right down over its toes, but as it eats its prey whole, the feathered feet are not fouled with blood. On the other hand, fish-eating owls have the usual bare feet and the same rasp underfoot as other birds of prey that live on fish. As the fish are not always eaten whole the scales would present a problem to feathered toes.

It looks quite effortless for some of the giant birds to float among the clouds and soar in the wind, but they rest for many hours to make up for one hour of flying. A vulture usually has to cover great distances before food is sighted, during which time its wings have to be held rigid to accommodate to the wind. For a true hunter there is the consuming concentration of swooping in at great speed and carrying off the prey. For those that hover there is the tiring, constant movement of wings. For those like the falcon there is the quick flight in, over and over again, until the pursuit is successful.

Predators use the wind. The sun burning into sheltered valleys or plains causes hot air to rise up into currents, or thermals, that spiral high into the sky. Wings tilted correctly into them carry the bird aloft without the necessity to flap. So well do they judge distance and wind direction, they know the exact height at which to soar in order to start and complete a long journey without once having to flap a wing. Most predators prefer to conserve effort by hunting prey smaller than themselves. But during a drought or when, for any other reason, food is scarce, they resort to knocking off from krantzes or rock ledges animals larger than themselves, and pounce upon them as they lie injured or dead on the rocks below. A predator's first targets are usually animals vulnerably young, old or maimed.

A large bird of prey has phenomenal eyes. Its vision has a quick change of focus so that the margin for error is minimized as it zooms rapidly toward its goal and is able to pinpoint the exact spots to sink in its talons, then soar up to the heights once again. Its eyes can turn in all directions, enabling it to see behind without turning its head.

It is estimated that the eye power of a bird of prey is about four times that of a human. A man could probably identify a guinea fowl about 600 yards away; an eagle's eyes would pick it up at about 1 1/2 miles away. A vulture, soaring higher, will widen the vision area to about 5 miles, especially since the food it seeks is a carcass that is large and more easily visible. Predators soar at about 2,000 to 5,000 feet, but at this height they are not looking for food; to do this, they come much lower. They soar to great heights when intending to start on a long glide toward a distant destination. A vulture glides effortlessly at 70 miles per hour, increasing to about 90 as it sights food. An eagle plunges down on its food with devastating accuracy, traveling at over 100 miles per hour. Some of the smaller aerial hunters are known to pursue their kill at about 200 miles per hour.

Apart from its extraordinary three-dimension ears, which would allow it to hunt by sound alone, the owl has eyes so big that they can barely turn in their sockets. To compensate for this limitation, the owl has the ability to turn its head right around. Not only can it then see in all directions with its night eyes, but also sounds are picked up by its ears, positioned in different places on each side of the head as it revolves.

The order Falconiformes covers a great diversity of birds of prey, from the largest—the Andean condor, with a wingspan of over 10 feet and an average weight of 25 pounds—to the tiny falcon that weighs about an ounce. Many of the larger ones can go for over a week without food, the smaller species needing food more often. An eagle weighing 9 pounds and possessing a wingspan of 6 to 7 feet needs about 4 pounds of food per week, while a 2-ounce falcon consumes a little over 6 ounces per week.

The male bird of prey is usually smaller than his mate; and in some species the female is twice his weight. The usual practice is for each partner to share any food with the other. The difference in their sizes allows for a greater diversity of prey. The smaller, quicker male tackles small, fast-moving animals while the female goes after the larger ones. The female is the larger because, as the stronger character and the more dominant partner, she keeps the home together and is the axis on which the survival of her species depends.

Fatherhood to the male is not the intense, consuming responsibility that motherhood is to the female. He is sometimes loath to give up food he has had difficulty in finding, even to his offspring. The size of his mate ensures her ability to wrest it from him for their babies, if necessary. The father's kills are adequate for the needs of the chicks when they are first born, for the victims are small and the food tender, but, once the babies start their rapid development, only the mother's powerful hunting skill can provide sufficient food for all of them. The mother broods the eggs and cares for the newly-born eaglets almost exclusively, and the parent on the nest is the defender against would-be enemies. Better, then, that it is the aggressive, stronger female that is in charge at this time.

Aquila verreauxi is known in South Africa as the black eagle, Witkruis arend (white cross eagle), Dassie-vanger (dassie catcher) and, by the Zulus, as Ukozi. A majestic eagle, pure black except for its white back feathers, which form a distinctive V when the wings are folded, it is found now only in the mountain fastnesses and is not often seen. The wingspan of a mature bird averages 6 feet for the male, and 7 for the female, though naturally individual sizes differ. Their respective weights are about 10 and 12 pounds and they stand about 3 feet. Yellow, hooded eyelids cover brown eyes, the beak is beige and feet yellow.

An eagle faces the usual hazards of a predator—injury, infected feet, torn talons, broken or deformed beaks and, most fatal, broken wings, all of which render it useless as a hunter and provider of food. But the decline in numbers is due mainly, despite a fine for their destruction, to persecution by man—his misapprehension that they take his lambs in large numbers, and the pushing of his progress into the natural world of a predator, disturbing the ecological balance and space needed for a bird of prey to survive. A pair of eagles requires at least 200 square miles of hunting territory. Black eagles live mainly on dassies (hyrax), and their domain includes several rocky stretches inhabited by these little mammals.

Only about a quarter of the eaglets born live through their first flying year. Tossed into the pitiless world of the wild when a few months old, they are killed or die of starvation, quite often because they are unsuccessful in finding an unoccupied territory where they can hunt. The skill of hunting has to be learned, practiced, improved on by trial and error. Quite often an eaglet despairs and dies—wounded in both body and spirit—from constant hounding and harrying by irate adults onto whose lands it has unwittingly ventured to find food. As with humans, there are good parents and some not so good, and an eaglet has a distinct advantage if its parents are conscientious, patient teachers. Not only will it be ready to face its ruthless world so well fed that layers of fat will tide it over the hungry days of trying to hunt on its own, but it will also have been well taught, thoroughly trained and disciplined.

Some eaglets, like their human counterparts, are inept, lack concentration and drive, are too gentle or too lazy to have much hope of surviving. But, whereas a human child's parents are prepared to provide for it and protect it no matter how it turns out, there are no such compensations for the wayward or weak eaglet. Unless it learns fast and well while its meager kills are supplemented by those of its parents, it will be ill-equipped to battle in a stark and hungry world. And, if it is injured in any way during this period, this is quite fatal, for no one will look after it. Sometimes, if a youngster appears to flounder when it is introduced to the great unknown, one of the parents will stay with it and try to get it established in a fairly unmolested territory. But not for long. Seven or eight months after it hatches out of the egg it is completely on its own. By then the parents are already turning to preparation for the next eaglet. The current eaglet, so possessively important to its mother for eight months, is now eclipsed by thought of the offspring to come.

A black eagle's aerial displays are some of the most spectacular of all predators. During the nuptial flights, the sky is filled with intricate evidence of their wooing. Their whole flying repertoire comes into play, breathtakingly beautiful. Their talons locked, their wings forming large, rigid sails, they roll over and over, their feet joined, riding the wind like a king-size box kite. The wind is their slave, to beat against or caress—a servant to carry them in their flight.

It is recorded that black eagles are silent birds that do not attack humans or draw attention to themselves. If that be so, those we came to know so well—and especially a certain female—must surely have been atypical of their species. She had a raucous voice which she used often, calling constantly as she watched us climb the mountain. She was fearless and highly intelligent, attacking us continually, yet quite prepared to bargain for the food we brought as though she recognized that we did not represent harm to her family.

Our black eagles were birds of prey that resented our coming to their world, yet accepted our being there. We were humans grateful to be there. They remained wild, instinctive predators. They did not change their makeup, nor did we. And, had we not all been completely ourselves, reacting in our different ways, there would not have been a story!

Friends Give Promise of Special Eagles

Each to his choice,
And I rejoice . . .
    KIPLING

Dawn and Arthur Bowland, like my family, have always loved being in the "Berg." That is where I met them, a few years before I climbed the Bell, and in the same part of the Drakensberg, at Cathedral Peak.

Arthur was chief photographer on Durban's morning newspaper, the *Natal Mercury*. A keen conservationist, he is famous for his wildlife pictures. He had a special interest in lammergeyer, a few pairs of which live in the Drakensberg. These great birds are truly kings of the heights, so we went looking for them in magnificent surroundings. Arthur and I developed a friendly rivalry. I appreciated that his birds were rare and impressive, but they were, after all, vultures, whereas my choice had the swift artistry of hunter birds. Eagles were less rare and smaller, but to me more exciting and beautiful.

Where Arthur thought there might be lammergeyer, there might likely be eagles, and often there were. Our searching was for us, and later for young Peter and Judy Bowland, a source of constant adventure and never-ending delight.

33

Arthur has a name, given by the Zulus, which roughly translated means "beer strainer." He often went on photographic assignments into Lesotho and knew many of the stories and legends of both Zulu and Basotho peoples, and the whereabouts of his birds.

He bargained with them for sheep and, with a carcass, tried to lure the big birds close in to his camera. Once he spent two days before a sheep changed hands, since it is neither polite nor indeed possible to hurry negotiations of this nature. Long conversations ensued during which the ancestors of the sheep's Basotho owners were discussed, and Arthur's own Yorkshire ones. Much beer had to be consumed. They found it difficult to understand that Arthur wanted to buy a sheep to hand out as a meal to the big birds.

"Before you get that sheep," I chaffed, "you are going to need that name of yours." Homemade Basotho beer is strong and coarse and can be heard thumping its potency day and night, as it brews in their huts.

From one camp in Natal Arthur bargained for a sheep, set up a hide, and waited for his lammergeyer. For many days he watched, to return one evening, his patience and tenacity a little worn. "There is everything in the sky," he said, "but they refuse to come in. They fly around . . . lammergeyer, Cape vultures, martial eagles. Even black eagles."

Arthur knew the area well and that evening he told me the history of the eagles that had at one time nested for many years on a particular mountain. His friend had known of them since he was a boy, eagles which had been mentioned in the farm's journal from the earliest days. Some had been killed, others driven away, their eggs stolen. And one gunman, believing that the eagles took his lambs, went up the mountain and riddled each egg with bullets. I found this unbelievable until, later on, I found bullet cases in the aerie, and I could imagine the distraught eagle parents pathetically turning over the shattered egg remains, before leaving the nest and the mountain. After some time they had returned, and then one of them was shot.

Every mountain has its legends. The farm with the eagle mountain as one of its boundaries had changed hands, and we wondered if the owner would be friend or foe of the eagles, and of us.

We met him, André, the next afternoon. He had seen the eagles fly over but had not yet been up the mountain. He had heard, too, of the farmers who believed that the eagles were responsible for their loss of lambs and shot at them whenever they could. André himself was convinced that there were only a few days in the year when it was possible for the eagles to take lambs. This was when they were first born, but he felt sure that predators would not often come down to the plains to take them. By the time the sheep moved into the hills the lambs were quite big. "I have seen them take lambs that have died of cold," he told us, "but they have to live through winter too." He was embarrassed that a tough farmer could harbor such sentiments but, having gone so far, added, "Besides, I like to see them flying about up there. They look so good." A friend!

His family and laborers were to watch us often, shaking their heads in disbelief as week after week we lugged up heavy packs, faced intense cold and lashing gales just to be with the eagles. Without André and the welcome at his farm, we should have achieved little. Often as I looked up at the eagles soaring above a farm where they were safe, I found myself thinking, "Thank you, André . . ."

It was late when we set out up the mountain, too late to reach the summit, but whenever I think of it I see it as it was that evening. It thrust over 7,000 feet above sea level, from a golden plain, like a squat candle guttering lower on one side, slabs of rock tilting together at the top to form a flame ignited by the last rays of the sun. On the rock face, patterned in with the shadows, we could make out a blur of untidy sticks.

I lagged behind in the dying day, thinking of past eagles, wondering what these would be like. Young Peter Bowland joined me. "What's that up there?" I asked. We stared at the summit. The rocks of flame looked like a Viking ship cutting its way through a sea of burning storm clouds. Even as we stood, a hail storm sent us skeltering down into the valley.

The last picture we had was of a celestial ship drifting into the sunset. When we looked back a little later the magic had gone. The mountain reared, a mass of cold stone, dark against the mist and hail and there was no sign of the proud eagle figurehead we had so clearly seen.

I am glad I did not see the mountain come to life then; glad the eagles did not soar into my life on a sunless day with all color drained from the world.

A Search Ends, and a
Warning Is Given

She was a form of life and light,
That, seen, became a part of sight;
And rose, where'er I turn'd my eye,
The morning star of memory . . .
                    BYRON

For the Greeks and Romans, the eagle was the symbol of fearless-
ness and freedom, a royal bird, sacred to Zeus and Jupiter. When
an emperor died, his soul was entrusted to a liberated eagle to
conduct it to the clouds. This strong association with the gods
ensured that it was only the eagle that could not be struck and killed
by lightning.

I hoped this was true.

The next morning when we set out we could not see the mountain. The far peaks were beset by a bonfire in the sky that tossed up
the clouds with forked lightning, letting the chaff fall in mist and
fine rain. If there were eagles up there, they would surely need the
protection of the gods.

We said little. The going was demanding and the frosty air cut at
our lungs. By the time we reached the plateau the sun had broken
through the tangled bonds of writhing mist, and the featureless
world was struck to gold by its power as it leaped from one dark

37

outline to the next, giving it form and substance. The sun lunged at the rock face but the mist refused to surrender the summit. It lay across the escarpment in white defiance and the sun, momentarily arrested, flooded back to our feet. It attacked once again, the mist quivered and, having shown signs of giving in, was soon put to rout.

The earth, a clumsy confusion of granite strength, seemed ostentatious against the gleaming, clean lines of the sky now that the sun had won. But for me its triumph went unheeded. I had eyes for nothing but the two black eagles pinioned in the sky. They were the most beautiful things I had ever seen.

That moment canceled out the years of waiting, and I knew, as one does, that a search was over and something was just beginning, for these were special eagles.

We toiled up. As the shadows of their wings fell across us, I had the sensation of being crucified. They swung above us, only their heads moving as they watched us, as if they held the strings to marionettes that jigged and jogged among the rocks to their superior will and dexterous, manipulating talons. It seemed they dangled us against the mountainside, letting us plod up, unsuspecting. When we breasted the rim, it was as if they let the strings drop as we fell in heaps of packs and tired limbs.

"Look out!"

Instinctively I ducked, but felt my sweater tented up from my back as a fury of feathers and talons whipped over me. I rolled back from the edge and searched the sky. "Come on," shouted Arthur, "it's coming in again. Come on . . . ," he bellowed as the black outline swooped again. We made a dive for the dubious protection of a large boulder and watched the eagle pair circling above.

Arthur looked at me. "What about your great eagles now," he asked with a grin, "and your poetic thoughts about them?" I had no answer. It was true that I had imbued them with the aura of gods. But contact was suddenly harsh and real. There was no mystery anymore. They were creatures of strength and purpose who did not like humans in their world.

After their show of power, they flew off in graceful duet and left us alone. But they had given us fair warning and something to think about. Ever after, the steep gully that needled its way up from the back of the wide plateau to the tip of the escarpment was the dividing line between the territory claimed by the eagles and that of the humans. This narrow track of crumbling rock was the only way to negotiate the sheer rock massif that ran along the aerie side of the mountain. Beyond this we were trespassers—to be prosecuted with rough eagle justice. No sooner did we approach the base rocks than two black outlines hung above us, watching, waiting, often appearing miraculously from a sky we were convinced was devoid of movement. Immediately we set foot in their realm, the female, the larger of the two, plunged into the attack while the male circled above. Not once did this pattern change. They always appeared at the gully when we arrived there.

She flew over again, dipping in toward us, purposeful, disdainful, shrugging off thought of peril; and, seeing us still against the rock, made for the summit to watch us from there. I looked at her closely. This was no ordinary eagle. She was unusually large and obviously old, much older than her sleek young mate. Compared to him, she was like a battle-scarred aircraft that had never lost a fight. She was proudly beautiful. "Everyone is as God made him," I quoted aloud, "and very often worse." The Creator had made a wonderful job of these eagles. But who had made this one worse? "I would be much worse," I supposed, "if someone came nosing into my property looking as if they were set to stay." Arthur agreed with me, adding, "It is a pity we cannot tell her we mean no harm."

An Eaglet Has Greatness Thrust Upon Him

*. . . why may not imagination trace
the noble dust of Alexander . . .*
SHAKESPEARE

Arthur kept watch over me and I peered over the edge, perched precariously overlooking a vast mountain country where a careless move would tumble us into a void and onto rocks hundreds of feet below on the plateau.

An almost fully grown eaglet stared at me from the aerie. He stood, all eagle in shape, his feathers the browns and russets of an adolescent nearly ready to fly. My delight knew no bounds and I called to Arthur, "He's great, a great little eaglet." And so we called him Alexander . . . the Great.

Not three months old, he looked poised enough to face the hazardous world before him, waiting patiently on the aerie. Yet somehow, to me, he was ill-equipped to handle the perils that would surround him. He lacked the signs of latent strength and ferocity I thought essential in an eagle. Because he would so soon have to fend for himself, the mother eagle's attacks were not as

41

intense as in two subsequent eaglets' early days. After the initial burst at the gully she was spasmodic in interfering with our walk along the escarpment to the clump of stunted trees and boulders we called "base." This was the only protection we had from the blazing sun, blinding snow, relentless wind and the attacking eagles.

In the few weeks we had of getting to know Alexander and his parents, our days were filled with surprise and interest. Innocents in a predators' world, we foolishly thought that all we had to do was to set up cameras and the eagles would know exactly what was required of them and perform accordingly. But, of course, it was not like that at all.

We were no newcomers to bleak mountain winters, but there was no shelter from the cold, no respite from the flagellation of the icy wind that was born on that mountain, lived there, but never died. The wind was a living thing that lay in wait, grabbed at us with fingers of cold steel, knocked us off balance and numbed our senses. I wished it could have been our ally. It was, instead, forever on the side of the eagles.

The rock face gave no promise of a permanent "hide," as far as we could see, and we were loathe to disturb Alexander when it was so near his time to fly. The wind, too, had a say in the matter; a hide could only be anchored with its approval.

Arthur, ingenious and dedicated, fashioned a radio camera. The idea was to settle the box on a ledge diagonally above the aerie and, from some distance away, be able to click the shutter at the right moment. Though he soon decided that his invention would not provide the success he was looking for, Peter and I were carried away with enthusiasm, especially as Alexander was a curious but unafraid observer of our efforts. With Peter beneath a makeshift skeleton tent of dead branches heaved up from the plateau, he and I looked as though we were on a fishing trip as we angled the box into position with the aid of two long rods and nylon thread. It was a job requiring endless patience, to be rewarded when we saw Arthur's pictures.

Perfectionist as he is in wildlife photography, he viewed the results as unsatisfactory compared to the pictures he had in mind; but, to Peter and me, the odds against getting them increased their greatness!

42

Perhaps it is just as well, though, that we did not pursue this method of photography. After settling the box, it meant returning down the gully to the plateau where Arthur held the controls. When the parents came into the aerie we could not be sure we had positioned the angle of the box correctly, and very often the strong wind shifted it. My journeys up and down took longer as the day wore on. I tried hiding at the base, but there was no doubt at all that the eagles knew I was there, and unless we were all on the plateau, they refused to fly to the aerie.

Peter did not always join us on the long rugged journey from Durban to the mountain. When he did, he and I revelled in the discovery of insects, flowers, and the special birds and animals in the vicinity of the mountain. To Arthur, consumed with devising a way to get close to his subject, the journey was a photographic mission. If his picture is of a deer, it is soft and delicate, the liquid eyes plead against violence. His rhinos are square and bad-tempered, flies crawl over prehistoric faces, and they look at you from anachronistic, short-sighted eyes. Giraffes caught in his lens stand with arresting ungainliness, their patterned necks hoisting astonishing heads with faces that seem perpetually astonished. Here now before him was the frustration of seeing wonderful material, yet being unable to come to grips with it, to focus his camera close up on it all—an eaglet, its fierce mother and aristo-cratic father.

Time was running out. Alexander was introduced to his world and his training began far from the aerie. The eagles, not bound to the mountain face any longer, flew farther and farther afield. Then they were gone altogether.

I knew that I would be back next year if the eagles returned to nest. Then the sky would pulse with the beating of giant wings as they made claim to their territory.

The Bonds Draw
Tighter

By viewing nature, nature's handmaid, art,
Makes mighty things from small beginnings grow . . .
DRYDEN

The following year, at the end of May, I went up the mountain alone. I took a long time getting past the eagles' vigilance but eventually managed a glance down at the aerie. There were two eggs—two for the sake of one.

Only one held the eaglet destined to live. I looked, wondering which would survive the seemingly senseless act of nature that allows only one egg to play a part in perpetuating the black eagle species. Even if both eggs hatched, only one chick would live. The stronger of the two would either starve out the weaker by pushing forward to get all the food and attention, or it would harry it to death. Or the mother, as soon as she was sure of one healthy offspring, would get rid of the remaining egg before it hatched.

It seemed an appalling waste, especially as the world is not overrun by black eagles. For over forty days both eggs would have the mother's warmth. For nearly six weeks the pulse of life would throb equally in each. A crack migh appear in both eggs to let in the light from the world into which each eaglet hoped to venture.

But only one of them would spread its wings in the blue of the sky above.

Arthur had been undecided about returning to the eagle mountain since the difficulty of maneuvering camera and a hide seemed insurmountable, and he was not prepared to compromise on the eagle pictures he wanted.

Peter, with his widening schoolboy interests, would not, I knew, be a regular companion; and, when he was able to accompany me, would I be able to look after myself and also keep an eye on an adventurous schoolboy?

I told them of the two eggs in the nest. Peter was delighted. Arthur could not resist the thought of another eaglet, another chance. I could barely wait. It was the last week of May and, until the beginning of July, when the eggs would hatch, we kept away.

Something of *Antony and Cleopatra* kept recurring:

> *Who seeks and will not take when once*
> *'tis offered, shall never find it more . . .*

All around me it was offered. Grateful, I held out my hands to it.

> *. . . That lightly draws its breath,*
> *And feels its life in every limb . . .*
>   WORDSWORTH

Cleo was born on July 3. On that day snow fell heavily. In the first light, the mountain was a gleaming castle. In May, the old lady of the mountain had given me tangible proof of her determination and tenacity in guarding it. Arthur wondered now whether we might disturb them to a point of no return. I recounted my lone journey to see the eggs, when I was conscious of being a very small human in a wide world ruled by eagles. I knew that if anyone should be frightened away, it would doubtless be us!

I could not believe that with all the hardship they would have to face they would easily give up and leave their chick behind. It was obvious in every line of the mother that she was made of sterner stuff than flying away because of us.

Now, in this our second year of being there, we sat in the scant shelter of the base about twenty yards from the lip of the escarpment, below which was the aerie. I could get nowhere near it. The two eagles sat on the summit rocks, and each time I made a move the female plunged down at me. After a while she glided off, but I was not convinced that her absence meant safety. I had made mistakes last year. So we waited.

During his mate's absence, we had to smile at the male. He was worried that he might not be able to cope with us, for he had apparently been left in charge, and his relief when he flew to meet her was quite obvious. I had just started to make a dash to the edge of the escarpment when Arthur said, "You've no chance now, look up there."

She came gliding round the shoulder with a green twig in her beak. Not in anyone's imagination did she resemble a dove of peace, but she was oddly touching as she brought in this spray of leaves of almost oriental delicacy splashed against her strong black outline. More poignant still was the manifest pride in the bearing of the token. She circled then dropped, with no hesitation or glance at us, to the aerie, and after a few moments appeared without the twig.

We did not know it then, but that green twig was filled with meaning. It was a sign that an eaglet had been born. As the eaglet grew, we were to see her bring them in often. Identified as *Maytenus acuminata*, the sprigs served to protect the baby from flies and sun and to freshen the nest. The bearing of these leaves was the only time I ever saw the eagles use their beaks for carrying; they lifted their prey with their talons.

From the plateau I had noticed a narrow ledge running above what looked like an old aerie site and, judging my time, I ran to the edge of the escarpment and slithered down onto it. Immediately the mother's shadow completely covered me as she hung above in the wind. Sometimes she dove down at me and tried to wangle me out with her talons, but my size allowed me to curl against the slight overhang and this prevented her from a good strike. She defended her home patiently, without frenzy, as though she knew her power, and that she only had to wait until I made a false move.

Arthur started to stroll up the slope and her concentration shifted to him for a spell. I inched out, fighting the wind, and caught a glimpse of the nest. Next to the egg, mottled with maroon blotches, lay a tiny chick. It had hatched from the rounder, plainer egg, and I wondered if it knew how lucky it was. I watched, spellbound, as it squirmed and squeaked in the basin of the aerie, not believing it could belong to the eagles. It looked so tiny and feeble to be the beginning of a giant, but the remains of a hyrax next to it reminded me of its predator heritage. Then my time was over as I heard the scream of the mother over me.

Eager to tell of the good news, I hauled myself up over the escarpment. A wing tip slashed across my neck again and again. The third time, I just beat it to the base. "Cleopatra has been born," I panted, "but she is certainly well guarded."

We had found a large dead hare on the road on our way from Durban, and we left this on the summit and went away, leaving baby Cleo to the care of her proud parents.

For the next few weeks snow, hail, rain and gales lashed the Drakensberg. When we were able to return, my glimpse of Cleo was that of a fat, woolly eaglet, eyes wide and alert. From then on, every Saturday until November we left Durban when the morning star was still bright in the sky, and after a day on the mountain completed the round trip of over two hundred miles. We spent weekends there, and all our leave-time, the Bowlands in their caravan in the valley at the foot of the mountain.

The view from my sleeping bag under the stars was one of unending beauty, especially when the snow crept down the slopes, or when high on the plateau I wakened to the hush of a lonely but peaceful dawn.

> Everyone has inside himself . . . what shall
> I call it? A piece of good news! Everyone
> is . . . a very great, very important character . . .
>
> UGO BETTI

Cleo's year taught us a great deal. We were in the same world as the legendary eagle that was vitally, fearlessly alive. Our eagle family began to have distinct personalities, and the female and I developed a close, turbulent relationship. I admired her tremendously. She was so every inch a creature of the wild. Her life allowed of no compromise. Her wisdom must have told her we did not threaten her family, but her instinct was not prepared to take any chances. Her great body gave mute evidence of how devotedly she guarded her own. She had a torn talon. Her right trousered leg appeared scarred, and one of her wings was singed along the top. Arthur reckoned her wingspan to be all of eight feet across. Spread over me, her wings seemed more than three feet wider than my height of five foot two.

Lights flashed in her splendid eyes and I often quailed before their gaze. She reminded me of an old schoolteacher I once had, her nose hooked over like this eagle's beak, her greying hair and dark, austere eyes giving her the distinct aquiline look. I had respect for her, too, and was grateful to her; for she had forced into a reluctant schoolgirl what was to become a great joy in poetry and literature.

I know that I credited this superb huntress with powers of reasoning, thought and intelligence that scientists and ornithologists will assure me she does not have. I can only say what happened, how our wild friendship grew.

Every day brought new proof of her knowing me, every encounter with her was evidence that she figured things out. The process was too deep and sometimes far too complex for it to be mere instinctive reaction. And no one will convince me that the tenuous current of understanding growing so steadily between us did not exist. It did! We knew each other, that wonderful old eagle and I. Our rugged friendship was flung across two worlds, hers and mine. It may not have had the proximity enjoyed by normal friends, but the friendship was strongly, surely there.

The male was very young, obviously not her first mate, for the disparity in age was too great. He was sleek and groomed and much smaller. He was wary of us and sensitive to his mate's slightest displeasure. He wove patterns of concern around us but never actually dived in except once, when, ignoring him, I turned my back when he was very near. But our mutual surprise at this unexpected daring so demoralized him that he never did it again. When I walked toward the eagle pair as they sat on their favorite rocks, the female waited until I was within a few yards of her. The male was not so bold and flew off almost as soon as he saw me start out.

From an early age, Cleo was just like her mother. There was no way for me to tell the sex of the eagles—even in adults their markings are exactly the same. The only difference is in their size.

49

But this baby was aggressively female. From the start she was large, plump and very bossy. The larger she grew the more she ruled the roost, ordering her food, elbowing her way around the aerie, shouting her temper.

She was as fiercely female as Alexander had been quietly male. Even her mother seemed exasperated by such a domineering, demanding offspring. As the months passed, she seemed to resemble an emergent teenager, difficult and wayward. But, for all her brash swagger she was, after all, only a few months old. I had the feeling she would be much better at survival than gentle Alexander, and could visualize her throwing herself into her training days with abandoned vigor.

They were truly very great, very important characters!

> *Progress, therefore, is not an accident,*
> *but a necessity . . . it is a part of nature . . .*
> SPENCER

We learned many things. Arthur followed the breathtaking flight of our black giants and worked out ways and means to get nearer to Cleopatra. To photograph eagles flying at over one hundred miles an hour requires more than pressing a button in calm, split-second timing. With his eye on the camera he brooked no interference from anyone, and he had a workmanlike attitude toward the demanding task he had set himself, giving early indication that while he had high regard for these great birds he would protect himself against any unexpected attack.

He wielded a short stick above his head as a warning. The female could not stand this display of power by anyone else. I am sure she knew that Arthur meant no harm, sure that she took pure delight in trying to catch him when he was undefended.

One day, Arthur was viewing the possibility of photography from along the edge of the escarpment. I was idly watching the female from the base and was prompted to shout out to Arthur, "You had better be careful. I have a feeling this is an 'I-hate-men' day." I could tell she was full of suppressed eagerness to swing down at Arthur, who was temporarily without his stick. "She has you in her sights," I warned again. "It is a very good flying day!" The black form dropped, and dove in, leaving behind her a healthy tear in Arthur's shirt. He swung round, furious. "The bitch got me!" he shouted, incredulous, and I laughed, surely not mistaken that her whole being spelled triumph!

With these eagles there was no contact, no way of communication. With a horse or a dog, or even a wild animal, a hand on its back transmits love, fear, danger, brutality. But there was the sky between this old eagle and me.

I talked about it to my parents, who were wise in the ways of the wild. "You have only yourself," said Dad. "She will have to know from your whole outline, your special aura that each human has, that what you feel for her is love and compassion. You will have to be a one-woman promoter for you, and the whole human race, for that matter. You will have to stand there and make every gesture, action, sound of your voice, talk to her."

I did not have her strength of character. She never weakened for a second, was always true to her eagle code. The sheer poetry of her often relaxed my guard in the face of such beauty. I gavn her openings for which she waited. I made mistakes. But she did not— ever.

I watched her flying and from it learned my only defense: to read the wind. After a while, by assessing direction and velocity, I could decide whether merely to incline my head, duck, fling myself on the ground or make a run for it when she rushed down to the attack. Once in the arc of her flight she had restricted maneuverability with her large wings and she could not change this at a moment's notice. She came in at my head, and by watching the beginning of her downward plunge I could swiftly work out, from the way and level they were directed at me, how to evade the razor talons. She connected a few times, but these were the result of my carelessness and her quick reactions.

Did she wonder about me? I aimed no gun, waved no stick, offered no resistance, did not retaliate. I was no threat to her home and baby, and I brought her food despite her ingratitude. Were her actions so part of her eagle metabolism, experience imprinted so bitterly on her, that humans brought forth the immediate need to attack? She was quite different in her approaches to Arthur. Were our outlines, then, so different, our auras not the same?

There was no doubt Arthur and I approached the whole project differently, that our sense of reward was not the same. Both of us would have gone to great lengths to protect her. How, then, could she go deeper than this? Men wiser than I probably have the answers. But, again, this was no ordinary eagle. She could not be neatly tagged or analyzed. She was a complete law unto herself.

We did a reconnaisance of the rock face to assess the possibility of a hide. Braced against the wind as I sat on the escarpment edge, the only protection I had was our rucksacks piled against my back. Arthur was on the end of the rope with a healthy drop beneath him as I belayed him, waiting in the icy atmosphere for his instructions.

Behind and above me was a powerful eagle, her line of attack stretched out like an invisible rope with a flawless connection. I teetered in the middle of human and eagle, and as she rushed down over me again, I felt as though I was a part of a moving rope, like a Yo-Yo.

Arthur decided that the old ledge might make a solid enough base for a photographer, so we moved into position above it. The old mother made the most of it as, with both hands occupied, I concentrated on getting Arthur down. The wind skimmed up and over the precipice and hurled pebbles into my eyes, while I tried to anticipate each move made by both Arthur and the eagle. At last Arthur was down.

He had given me instructions. "When I get my camera set up, secure the rope. Then, when I am ready, I'll shout and you put the dead rabbit on the very edge of the rim above the aerie. I am not going to be able to see what is going on up there. So when the eagle looks as though she might dive down at the rabbit, you must let me know. Then I'll be able to anticipate it as she swoops in to take it. I want this picture against the skyline and every second will count."

I was so dumbfounded at this casual list of instructions, me on a sheer rock face, an eagle mother at her most provocative above, and at the task of keeping up a running commentary on her movements that I obeyed without protest. I was not sure that she'd come in at all.

But she did. "She's getting ready to dive," I shouted. Then, suddenly, "Now!" as she roared over, so close that the lens of the camera picked up every feather of her splendid wings as she took the food.

Arthur's picture was a masterpiece.

I was quite sure he would be satisfied, but I had not realized the depth of purpose when a photographer has set his mind on a special picture. He dearly wanted one of the eagle mother and her child. The hide Arthur constructed was a plaything in the wind, unless we found some better means to anchor and strengthen it.

Cleo was growing fast, and the weeks were passing rapidly. Our time on the mountain seemed to be made up of dashing out of the way of eagles and wind to the aerie to see Cleo, and learning to evade talons and gale. We began to be quite adept at this, almost without knowing it.

O! what a deal of scorn looks beautiful
in the contempt and anger of his lip . . .
SHAKESPEARE

His mind alive to every possibility, Arthur decided to try the "out of sight out of mind" theory. One Saturday after I had belayed him to the ledge, he crouched there under an old blanket waiting for the mother eagle to cooperate and come in to her baby. I had a very high opinion of the eagle's intelligence and told Arthur I would not be surprised if she came in and lifted the blanket off his back! But everything was worth a chance. He thought that if I lowered the rabbit onto a ledge near the aerie the mother would not be able to resist it.

For a while the mother was not concerned with the aerie. I had her undivided attention as I first maneuvered Arthur and then the rabbit down to their ledges. I often talked up to her, shouting a welcome when we arrived and when I tried to entice her in for food by holding it up in my hand. Now I said, "Come on, it's just part of a photo. You only have to fly in and get it." She shouted back at me, and I could only make a conjecture as to its translation.

I could not see Arthur, but I could hear the muffled impatience coming up from the ledge. "You two dames had better work out something quickly," he said, "or I'll fall off this ledge."

I looked down at him and laughed. "She'll never believe that blanket act. You *look* what you are, a guy under a blanket, and this old girl's much wiser than we are."

My merriment was sobered only by the sound of the truculent

53

photographer below and the waiting eagle above. I moved to the base away from the scene of action and left them to get on with it. The eagle immediately floated down to investigate.

The male joined her, but she suddenly called out to him and they rose together immediately above Arthur. She took in everything—the still form under the blanket, the rabbit on the ledge, me amongst the rocks at the base. She sped to the top of the mountain in preparation for her downward plunge, then gave up like a spent arrow, as though she'd had second thoughts about it. The attack turned into a casual glide.

She spread above us as she shouted encouragement to Cleo; cocked a glorious head at the rabbit, Arthur, me; called to her mate and, without a backward glance, rose into the sky and flew off. She must have felt a great many things, but her gesture of winging off into the void was one of eloquent contempt that we should under-estimate her. Clearly, the battle was not worth it if we stooped so low.

I was glad. And she was right. It was simply not "cricket," and she had shown her superiority by ignoring our clumsy attempts to outwit her. Demoralized, Arthur and I looked at each other and, with mutual consent, collected our things and walked down the mountain. The rabbit belonged to the eagles. And we knew it.

> *Be not afeard; the isle is full of noises,*
> *Sounds and sweet airs, that give delight*
> *and hurt not . . .*
>
> SHAKESPEARE

One day I took my tape recorder. Our packs were always heavy and any extra load had to be considered important to be included. However, I thought my parents would like to hear the appealing chant of the eaglet and the electrifying scream of her mother. The old people shared my firm belief that one day she would realize that the food I offered was from a human whose outline did not spell danger. When Arthur saw the tape recorder he concernedly chaffed me, "You're intent on killing yourself with luggage, aren't you?" and, halfway up the mountain, I thought him right, and very nearly ditched it then and there. But I am glad I persevered.

Those first tapes are a dramatic record of sounds from mountain, predators, humans. Sometimes, dodging talons, watching or belaying Arthur down to the hide or entranced with the flying of the eagles, I forgot the recorder was running and, when I played it back, the echoes of rumbling stones as I slithered to evade an attacking eagle, her raucous screams and the pithy comments from the humans invaded the tranquility of our home like a blast from another planet.

There was always the wind as background. There were sounds like a giant blundering along to the cacophony of screeches. There were words pitched with meaning: "Look out!" and "you two women had better sort things out . . . ," then, "she's flying in. . . ." And often, interspersed in the staccato warnings, involuntary curses and quick commands were paeans of praise: ". . . just look at her . . . just look at those glorious wings . . . ," and, "she's quite the most beautiful thing I know. . . ."

The eaglet calls plaintively, hungrily. Laughing doves coo-coo, falcons accompany their spinning with their calls, thunder booms. After one eagle scream and a crash at close quarters, there is silence, a succinct comment and the sound of a body rolling over and out.

Sometimes I played the sounds back to the eagles. The mother floated passively above, wondering at this strange human who could repeat the very things she had just shouted. And when the eaglet came on the air, she sped back and forth, not with anxiety but with interest, for she could see Cleo on the nest and could only wonder where the other eaglet was.

Subsequently, for our film, Peter became officer in charge of sound, and he taped on special equipment the screams, whistles and eaglet cheeps. He handled his task with patience and concentration and recorded the eaglet's piping voice to perfection. This was a difficult task, as the wind thrust its sound everywhere and the recorder picked up the slightest whisper, even the special whistle the female reserved for me as she made a grab at my back. In the comparative seclusion of the base, or sitting quietly down on the hide, he got on with his important and integral part of the mountain team.

*. . . And a pleasant thing it is for the eyes to
behold the sun . . .*

In mythology it was believed that when an eaglet was a few days old its mother held it up in her talons with its eyes directly to the strong rays of the sun. If it was unflinching and unblinking, it was favored, would live and be strong, while the unfortunate eaglet that blinked or turned away from the blazing light was virtually abandoned as having no chance of survival. This, it was also believed, was the reason that all living eagles can stare at the sun without effort or discomfort.

I had grown fond of my eagle family so I worried about the eaglets. Had Alexander drawn back from the sun's blinding rays? He had not been abandoned, but he had seemed far too much of a little gentleman to be facing the demanding life of an eagle.

"You are becoming involved," warned Arthur as I expressed my concern. "Of course I am," I agreed, not seeing any escape from it. "What are you?" I asked, curious to know what the picturemaker really felt. "A photographer," came the prompt reply! But I could not get to know an eaglet and just dismiss its fate without a thought.

I looked at Cleo. This one would have stared right back at the sun and found it challenging. Cleo, precocious and energetic, turned out to be even more forward than we had believed. I had watched her over the past few weeks as she strutted, then flapped her wings and ostentatiously jumped up and down to exercise her legs. I was sure it was just showing off. But when we went up one Saturday, the aerie was empty. Bossy little Cleo, who had grown so lovely and was looking forward with such enthusiasm to her life, had gone.

The mountain was silent. It watched us walk away. It knew us, eagles and humans, as we moved across its face. Now it had another secret, for part of me was left behind in its keeping.

56

"Merry Christmas!" and "Many Happy Returns"

And I shall have some peace there,
For peace comes dropping slow . . .
                    W. B. YEATS

The Bowland family had gone off to the Cape for the Christmas holidays. Arthur, with some wonderful pictures, was doubtful whether time and expense would allow a further five or six months in the coming year to make the long trip to the mountain every Saturday. But thought of the eagles and their beauty was constantly on the retina of my mind. It was December—midsummer in South Africa—so the giants would not be defending their territory so rigidly. The rock face was important when it held an eaglet in the aerie.

This time I went with Dad. He was in his ninetieth year and his grief for my mother was a gentle disbelief at a life without her, after well over fifty years together. We knew that the eagles had probably gone farther afield, but Dad was quite happy just to go to the mountains. He took his dog and took his time, wandering slowly among the boulders up to the plateau.

"I thought I could see your eagle world in my mind," he said quietly, "but it was nothing as lovely as this. . . ." The mountain had put on its best face and Dad, a keen botanist, gloried in its wealth. We had lunch in a hollow where flowers erupted in shoals of color to a cascading stream. There were many more birds about than I had noticed during the winter, and the butterflies were a riot in the blossoms.

Dad and I spent a happy few minutes trying to outdo each other in remembering the fascinating array of names given to the species of small warblers, one of which arrived unexpectedly on our lunch table rock, paused, startled out of action for a moment, then went off in shrill complaint. He was one of a large family—Cisticola— and the names of his relatives ranged from the high-sounding Le Vaillants to the Common Cisticola. In between there are cisticolas that are: Fantail, Desert, Pale-crowned, Spotted Cloud, Neddicky, Wailing, Tinkling, Rattling, Singing, Bleating, Dusky-faced, Grass-shopper, Moustache, Pinc-pinc, Zulu Reed, Red-faced, Chirping, Blackbacked, Croaking . . . right down to the Lazy Cisticola!

Another visitor was a Tinkie, quite at home in eagle landscape, where he achieved fame and his South African name. I could visualize this fragile little bird nestling, light as air, on the eagle's back as it soared higher and higher in the stakes for the title King of the Birds. The eagle was the undisputed lord of the skies. None could compete with his strength, none could fly higher than he! Then, when even he had reached his limit to claim, "I am he," a tiny clear voice piped from above, "No! It is I who am your king, for did not I go highest of all?"

We laughed at this impudent miniature as he brightly reminded us of the story himself, of how he bested the eagle to become King Tinkie. "He looks a wee king with a kroon on his head," smiled Dad, as the small monarch flitted about, all confidence and contentment, with his status and the day.

From the plateau, the ring of the Berg was like a crown. It had about it the strength of the eternal mountains covered in soft and purple comfort. It was a long way from the Highlands my Dad would never see again, but he soaked up the tall loveliness of the Drakensberg, and I could see his heart easing under the balm of it. His pure white hair rippled in the wind, and his eyes shone. And the sight, so long missing in his sadness, smiled away some of my grief, too.

While Dad drifted around in the wonderland of the plateau, I trudged up through the gully to take the two rabbits I had brought. I thought to put them on the escarpment as I had always done. I could not be sure that the eagles would find them, but how could I come to the mountain empty-handed? I left them on the soft turf slope, then went to look at the aerie. It was a garden! Wild lilies with small white flowers were rife among the sticks. Wild cinnerarias had taken advantage of the rich compost to blaze into unseasonal purple blossoms.

Stillness was all around me. Summer clouds arched across the afternoon sky as I joined Dad, and we wandered down to have tea with my Zulu friends at the foot of the mountain. With the innate courtesy of their race, these people had always forborne to comment when, in all weathers, Arthur and I went to photograph the big birds of heaven country. They and I gravely exchanged gifts each week. I took them provisions, clothing and new bread, and was presented, in turn, with fresh brown eggs.

Once when I arrived from the mountain top I found a large rooster trussed up, ready for me to take home. After diplomatic explanation I left him there, in his own home, free to run around among his numerous wives, but I became very fond of him and sought him out each time I returned.

Always I started off to the icy heights aglow with thought of the huts against the mountain, and the two friends and their four delightful children living there, who would let me warm my hands at their fire when I came back in the evening, numb and beaten by the wind.

Now, as always, I looked up. I expected nothing, not asking more than the fullness I felt on this rewarding day. But here in the land of the eagles, my head was ever thrown back to encompass the reality and possibility of what the sky might hold.

The eagles floated over the far ridge and made their graceful way along the escarpment, shimmering in the summer haze. My being surged with the joy of them. "Dad!" I cried. He stood, his eyes chipped from the blue of the sky as he watched the three eagles wing over. Cleo and her parents! When they reached the slope that held the rabbits they circled once or twice, then raced to the summit. For a few moments the three familiar outlines etched into the sky, then two of them bore down on the gifts. Cleo floated after them. They waited for her, then flew on over us.

"Merry Christmas!" I yelled, bursting with delight. And my heart soared with them as they looked down. "And many happy returns . . . ," Dad added. We laughed joyously, for this was always Dad's greeting to anyone, at any time of the year. He believed that each day was a wonderful one for someone. This time it was so right —many happy returns of this lovely day, indeed.

We watched the eagles ring up in the wind and disappear into the clouds. Then they were back again with the rabbits still clutched in their talons. Dad could not take his eyes from them, and I knew that he drank in the beauty of them for my mother, too. And how could anyone but be grateful for the priceless gift of those lovely wild giants to an old man so beloved.

Long after they had disappeared he stayed looking at the rapture of the sky that had held them. Then he looked at me, saying nothing, the sight of his face a miracle to me.

Never Two Without
a Third

The brave are born from the brave and good.
In steers and in horses is to be found the
excellence of their sires; nor do savage
eagles produce a peaceful dove . . .
                    HORACE

It was June in the third year of climbing the mountain. Winter was already upon the earth. Frost crackled underfoot as I made my lone way toward the plateau. The air was stunningly cold.

An eagle has the finest vision of any living creature. Still, I doubted if even the eyes of the black eagles I had come to find again could have penetrated the thick mist curling and heaving round me.

As I started up the slope the trees were shapeless shadows, entities different only, close up or by touch, in the distinctive patterns of the bark. Sometimes as I struggled for a foothold the huge boulders hunkering in ragged groups in the mist gave me very solid help. I longed for the sun, but the only sensation of warmth came from the sight of a miniature wild peach tree, with a

61

faulty notion of spring still months away. It was ahang with fragile pink blossoms. Then it, too, was swallowed up in the clammy gloom.

There was no sound, not even the amiable derision of the mocking chats that usually hopped from rock to rock to stay ahead of me.

After an hour's heavy going I reached the plateau and, although I could barely see a yard ahead, I had little difficulty in making my way to the large slab of rock that had a natural bonsai tree forcing its life from a deep crack. I did a mental calculation: I must have been up and down this mountain over forty times. Small wonder that the flat rock was familiar to me.

This was the point where, after the demanding haul up the bouldered slopes, I removed my rucksack and stopped to look at the splendor of the Drakensberg, letting my eyes wander round the circle of mighty snow-capped peaks until, finally, they rested on this mountain spur before me. Today the mist was a wall shutting out everything. I could only peer in the direction of the sheer rock face and wonder: had the eagles returned for the third successive year?

Through the swirling mist I caught glimpses of snow, and I knew every crevice would be packed with it, and that in the gully it would be thick and deep. I was on my own, and I would need every vestige of light and all my concentration to enable me to make my way up without the added thought of eagle shadows poised in the darkness, beyond my vision, for the downward attack. Quite often we found that the mist was confined to the foothills and plains, and that above the ridges and escarpment the summit rose clear into a sunny sky. But it would be asking for trouble to rely on this. I huddled on the rock, trying to evade the icy wind and trying, too, to convince myself that the prickly sensation down my spine was a rivulet of water that had found its way into my anorak, and not the strong feeling I had of being watched.

If the eagles had returned to take possession of their mountain and aerie to produce another chick, there would by now be eggs in the nest. And this is what I had come to find out.

Jamais deux sans trois, I kept convincing myself. Alexander and Cleo, and never two without a third. But, until the day cleared I would not know whether there was to be a third chance. Yet I had a feeling that the family on the rock face would, this year, give meaning to all the other eagles that had gone before. It was twelve years since I had come face to face with those on the Bell; three years since I had met this particular family.

I thought of what Arthur had said: "Would you be prepared to make a film with me?" My love for these eagles and particularly the obvious understanding between the old female and myself prompted him to capture it on celluloid. He knew that I could be the persuader of the eagle actress, that she knew me and would let me come closer to her; and that, if anyone could "sort things out" for a film, it would be the two women—eagle and human! I intended going up the mountain anyway, and I agreed wholeheartedly that the wild beauty of these mountain fliers was well worth sharing with others.

The mist changed to cloud, low down and fitful. Through a brief break I saw that the summit was white and that the sky above was like the Sistine Chapel where, as the clouds drifted and changed shape, I saw the finger of God giving life to man. The clouds swirled away taking the picture with them, part of the divine mystery remaining.

It was very early. A group of deer, luminous in the sun-drenched mist skulking in pockets on the plateau, bounded in front of me and I decided to follow them, away from the customary track up the gully.

I soon lost the deer—but found, instead, my eagle.

She called eerily from the mist, and the sound was directly above me. My heart hammered. She shouted again, as if chiding me for taking the wrong route. After all this time did I not know the way?

I shouted back incoherently, welcoming things, sentimental and glad, totally out of keeping with her wildness, but utterly in harmony with my happiness. The sun picked out her form from the greyness as she stood on a crag and I looked at this splendid creature, so known, so loved. She was a ruthless killer, yet had I not seen her crumple in tenderness for her chick? Had she not shown, in her own way that, despite her eagle makeup, she was trying to accept me? Clouds closed in, and, when I could see the crag again, she had gone. She had probably been watching me for a long time.

She had appeared to be tearing at something between her feet. My curiosity whetted, I left my rucksack and, after a few attempts, climbed up to where she had been standing. The sheltered ledges were sparkling with exquisite little flowers opening in the rising sun, in serene defiance of the snow a few feet away. It was a scary climb, but at length I pulled myself over the rim of the escarpment and landed on a heap of small animal skulls and abandoned feet.

A thick heathlike bush, shaped by the wind, spread low over the edge. It was full of mauve flowers similar to daisies, and the tightly-knit twigs, spiky leaves and golden-centered blossoms were garlanded with bits of fur, guinea fowl feathers and pieces of rabbit skin. In the middle was a macabre mixture of bones, fleshless heads of rabbits and hyraxes, and what seemed to be large rats. I scrambled up hastily from the gruesome spot, this butcher's block where the eagles decapitated their prey, tore through the skin and, if there was an eaglet on the aerie, took food back to it. The distance to the nest on the rock face was, I guessed, about a quarter of a mile, but not more than a few moments of direct eagle flying time.

The cloud and mist kept a protective sheet around me as I made my way down, and by the time I had made my way to the gully the day was in full swing. The sun was in complete control as it bestrode the earth like a colossus, aware of its terrible power as it rose inexorably in the sky. Its rays radiated like a mighty prayer wheel rippling splendor over the glistening snow.

The mother eagle, too, was in full swing. She cleaved the air with her great wings as she dropped, planed out into a glide as I started up the gully, then hung above me like an elegant hostess in the pristine world of blue sky and white earth, waiting for the butler to announce me.

Beauty does something different to each one of us. And this black eagle was beautiful. Just watching her taming the wind was a marvelous feeling—windswept, soaring and glad.

She dived, and I flattened against the rock, expecting her to keep her warnings up for some time, but she merely alighted on the summit and watched me toil up the gully. Two or three times she dropped down and floated over me, but somehow I knew intuitively that she was only looking at me. Long before I reached the escarpment, she had gone.

At the base I searched the sky. There were only a dozen vultures, very high above me. I wondered if I should risk taking a look at the aerie but realized that that was probably where she was. I sat back, loath to disturb her if she was on the nest. I waited, looking out over the mountain tops that were crowned with snow and at the orange glow of winter all around.

She shouted and the sound was very near. Then I saw her craning her neck round a rock near me. I laughed out loud at her inquisitive peeping, so out of character, and she jumped away, hissing. "This is your friend, remember?" I called, and at the sound of my voice she shot up, landed again, then waddled along, clumsy as a cowboy without his horse, her grace completely gone as she struggled on the alien medium of the earth. She positioned herself where she could see me, but was not on guard, and gave meticulous attention to her toilette. I could only presume that either the male was on the nest and this was one of her brief times away from the eggs, or that there were no eggs. As I had seen no sign of the male I hoped he *was* on the eggs. One thing I knew—if I made any move toward the escarpment, she would be in at me like a flash. It was difficult to believe, looking at her amicable proximity; but being a predator overwhelmed the compromise she was sometimes prepared to make toward me.

I studied her closely. She was following the dictates of her eagle makeup as I was following mine. I would want her to be fearless, with a savage caution to handle the dangers always waiting to leap out at every turn. I would want her to keep this mistrust of humans, for this was her defense. I did not want her to change. But she was so beautiful that I did not want the hatred coiled from bitter experience to be directed so unswervingly at me. I wanted her to know of my friendship. And, surprised, I realized that what I really wanted was to win the sanction of this eagle's approval.

Arthur had always been the rabbit provider. All I had been able to manage was one from the butcher. It was neatly skinned and wrapped up in a plastic bag. I demurred, hesitant about offering such a civilized gift, but it was better than nothing. I unwrapped it and set it on the grassy slope, and ducked as she came screaming in. The curve of her flight swerved her away from the rabbit and she circled over me as if wondering what I would do next.

"Sorry," I called, "but this is what's underneath all the other rabbits you have had. It will save you the bother of taking off the skin."

She called restlessly. "Come on," I shouted, "it's all yours." I stood quietly and she swung in lower, inspecting the pale-skinned food on the grass. Then she made for the summit and gathered her forces for the grab. As her talons hit the rabbit she seemed, fleetingly, to stall, as though surprised at what she felt. But she was all victory as she hoisted it aloft and made for the butcher's block.

She would not be long away and, when I saw the male rise from the rock face and follow her, I knew I had only a few seconds. I flung myself down and looked over the edge of the escarpment down to the aerie. Two eggs! Then I was off, running for the gully. I reached there just ahead of her, but only just.

When I looked back from the plateau she was on the nest and, on the block, the male had taken over the rabbit. She gazed down at me, relaxed and superior now that I offered not the slightest gobbet of disturbance or danger.

One of those eggs held my eaglet. The stage was set for getting to know this family well. They accepted us and were prepared to bargain with us. They would remain all eagle and the female, especially, would not swerve from her ferocity, but now, to me, it was reflex rather than pure aggression.

There was to be a third eaglet, and I was quietly grateful. From one of those eggs would come the resplendent wonder of an eagle. There would be no mediocrity in its early life, no flaw to threaten its ultimate perfection. It would be hewn from harshness, honed by the elements, scoured by hunger. But it would rise, unscathed, a monarch because of it.

To Mr. and Mrs.
Aquila Verreaux, a Son

He is born in a good hour
who gets a good name . . .
FIFTEENTH-CENTURY PROVERB

The eaglet would be very precious. Throughout her long life the old eagle had suffered heartache, denial and tragedy; yet, for the past two consecutive winters we had known her, she had hatched out an offspring. Now she was growing old. How long would it be before she was unable to hunt for her life, or before a domineering female came along ready to fight her for her young mate? How much longer would she be able to lay eggs, be able to play her rigorous part in the life of a black eagle? Every eaglet she hatched might well be her last. She sensed this and was prepared to guard each one with her life.

This year the eaglet would be precious to me, too, if it hatched and lived.

It was the first week in July and six weeks since I had seen the eggs. In a few hours I would know.

Snow flurried round our camp and clumps of grass were changed to sprays of glittering ice diamonds. A small spring seeping from the rocks hung in ropes of petrified pearls.

In the wind a flock of starlings bounced off course as though flung from a catapult. Bunches of sheep trotted under low, snow-laden branches, bleating their way to distant patches of grass.

As we started, the sun on the horizon soon left us far behind. The gully looked impassable. Battered by the climb, spirit and body seemed to resist the formidable little strip of mountain. I slipped and slid in the snow, scrabbling for a hold, and lay for a moment to rest.

We had expected the eagles at the gully, and were disappointed when the female did not dive in familiar pattern when we arrived. At least I would then know they were alive! Now, suddenly, she swung above me. I lay not knowing when the strike would come. Arthur's shout broke the hypnotic spell and I rolled clumsily over as a wingtip whisked up the snow. The wind screamed.

"She's always got something up her sleeve," Arthur said. I nodded, chilled. She had taken her time, arrogant in her confidence that whatever she meted out to us we would accept. I had thought that with my superior human mind I knew all her moods, knew her reflexes, had her actions taped. But what a store of knowledge about me she had stacked up!

Arthur had constructed a strong hide of hessian, but it was impossible to even try to position it; we would have been swept over the edge. Awful as the trip up had been, I had no intention of leaving without seeing the state of the eggs. The wind clawed at me with madman's hands, but I crawled to the rim.

The aerie was ahang with snow and I stared at it, not comprehending the damp and lifeless bunch of sticks that had such a short time ago held a neat basin with two eggs. There was nothing on it but an old carcass and snow.

"Something's happened," I faltered as I ran. "There's nothing there." I did not wait but floundered down the gully, my feet leaden with aching disappointment.

I looked up through a blur, from the plateau. The eagle twosome were keeping an eye on Arthur following me down, but after a while they flew off and were soon engulfed in an infinity of sky.

Would they return? Arthur was pessimistic. Why should they? In former years when something happened to the eggs or chick they had not come back. But, as I walked, I became cocooned in the absurd belief that despite the seeming finality of it all this was not the end.

We were here for a long weekend and the next morning we set off into a silent world of white. Nothing moved but drops of water as the molten lava of the sun melted through the snow. By the time we reached the plateau small globules of music were tinkling all around us. The sky was empty. The rock face was bare of the familiar black forms. We toiled up the gully. This was where the mat said "Welcome" in the language of the eagles. It was where we had begun to learn part of their rugged makeup, to become attuned to the sound of their calls. It was the dividing line, and there had always been a custodian demanding us to halt for recognition. Now it was nostalgically bare of eagle shadows, and the silence throbbed in our ears.

Then suddenly I was covering my head with my arms, and I saw Peter and Arthur roll away to the side. I looked up at the jetting giant and was glad. She was back. They had not gone away after all! But had they come back by mere habit, to challenge us at the gully?

The wind hurled itself at us as the sun came up, and the world glistened. It was glorious flying weather. The female was rampant, and even the male cruised up and down as I slid down to my ledge. Watching them made me forget the heartache that nagged at me. Looking at the disastrous aerie would be like probing a throbbing tooth.

I looked down. It was desolate. Wind tore at the blobs of snow and at the fur of the hyrax carcass. The dead twigs of a small bush scraped against the rock. The eagle charged past, shouting at me. I looked at the aerie, then back at her, and wondered at her anxiety. In the pocket of silence while the wind was suddenly still, nothing moved.

Nothing—except the fur of the hyrax—and it was not by the wind. I dared not breathe in case the illusion vanished. But there was no mistake, the carcass of the hyrax was moving.

And there it was, the eaglet, almost unmoving, but feebly trying to free itself of the dead hyrax pinning it down. Bedraggled and frozen with snow, it slowly pushed its way out. I looked, incredulous, at the grotesque scrap of life, all big feet, swollen eyes, all of it soaking wet and miserable, trying to raise a too-heavy head on a too-thin neck. It called, a thin, reedy cry for help.

It lived! And I knew, with a thundering in my ears, that my special eaglet had been born.

Riveted to the ledge, I found it impossible to grasp that this puny object would one day turn into a replica of his parents; that its feet, milk-white and soft, would produce the talons of a killer; that its beak would rip and tear and that those wing stubs would turn into flawless tools of flight.

Then came the powerful throb of wings and the thud of large feet on the nest. The female eagle had eyes for nothing but her baby. And for me the scene that followed was a fragment of perfection.

Gently pushing away the carcass with her beak, she gazed intently down at the eaglet. Its neck was too weak to lift its head as she nuzzled it tenderly and carefully probed for lice with her lethal beak round its closed eyes. She would not feed it until tomorrow, when it was stronger, and she seemed intent now on infusing it with the very will to live.

My mind was awhirl watching her, this wonderful giant whose love and strength would give the eaglet life. And I was caught up in the golden torrent of Roy Campbell's "Flaming Terrapin."

> . . . This sudden strength that catches up men's souls
> And rears them like giants in the sky,
> Giving them fins where the dark ocean rolls,
> And wings of eagles when the whirlwinds fly . . .

And I thought: if I drench my mind with the wonder of it, it will be there always, rich and rewarding. There would be the loveliness of the mother eagle as she bent down to her youngster, aware of the precious life of an ugly duckling that would one day spread its wonderful wings and ride the heavens.

Until that moment I had intended calling the eaglet Ukozi, which is Zulu for eagle. But that was now forgotten. A messenger of the skies, its mother, had winged in with a heaven-given name that came in a flash—Temujin—the boyhood name of Ghengis Khan, known as "Rider of Heaven." Temujin.

"Hello, little Temujin," I called down to him. He turned instinctively at the sound and, in my joy, I like to think it was acknowledgment of his christening.

The mother looked at me searchingly, as though aware of me for the first time. "Congratulations," I said, "and thank you."

As Temujin shifted slightly I caught sight of the remaining egg. I had had a bet with myself, and saw now that I had lost. I had been sure, somehow, that the eaglet would hatch from the more rounded, plainer egg, as Cleo had done. Cleo had had beside her a mottled egg similar to the one from which Temujin had now hatched. She had been undeniably female, a small replica of her mother in every way, and I wondered if the difference in shape and the markings on the eggs had any significance.

I swarmed up over the escarpment rim. Arthur and Peter could see the joy all over my face. "It's Family Day," I shouted, unable to hide my delight, "and Mr. and Mrs. Aquila Verreaux have a son. The boy is a little damp, but the whole family is fine."

"Some family," Arthur grinned broadly, thinking of Peter with us and the rest of his family waiting for him in the valley. We knew that Temujin would need the undisturbed attention of his parents, so we left our gift of food and wended our way down the mountain.

> *Yes; I am proud, I must be proud to see*
> *Men not afraid of God, afraid of me . . .*
> POPE

If I had expected any change, any spilling over onto me of the tenderness I had witnessed yesterday, I was mistaken. As I raced to my ledge a deafening screech rebounded from the rock face. I jumped down quickly and curled against the overhang. I had only one thing on my mind.

He was there. Alive, hungry, not beautiful, but very precious. "Hi, Temujin," I called.

His eyes could not see, I was sure. They looked as though they were covered with some kind of protective sac with only a pinpoint of an opening in the center. But he nodded in my direction, and I felt as though I had been given a gold mine. He was aware of shadows over him, but it is difficult to say whether he knew which belonged to his parents. He gave a little bob of his head as they passed over, but I noticed that there was the same reaction when two martial eagles glided over before they were quickly sent on their way by Temujin's father.

I whistled to him and he turned instantly. Then he continued his cheep-cheeping in the direction of the last shadow. That's where the food would come from, not from the odd sound coming from the ledge above him.

He was still safely snuggled in the basin and made no attempt to move. The wind came hunting round the mountain. Sometimes a gust caught at Temujin's head and he cheeped in alarm, and ducked down. He sat there quite alone. The plain egg had gone.

We were going to position the hide this morning, and I was suddenly guilty of being selfish, and of possibly wasting time, having my own few moments with my eaglet.

But I had waited a long time for the joy of being able to be part of his life, and nothing could take it away now. I thought of Cleo, of Alexander, with great affection. But what I felt for the diminutive travesty of an eagle before me now was something more. I had almost seen him born. He had been given back to me when I thought him dead. His mother and I were working out a mutual friendship, regardless of appearances.

I raised my head over the rim prior to making a dash back to base. But not even Arthur and his stick could stay the mother's tempestuous anger that I had blatantly disregarded her. I realized that although I must automatically have kept a conscious eye on the danger of her, my main thought had been to get to Temujin again. I had appeared to ignore her and her power, and like Arthur's stick, she hated it. . . . I tried to melt into the rock as she came in again and again. From the base, Arthur walked in a wide detour and put the rabbit we had brought on a slope some distance away. Only then did she give me a chance to escape.

Shaken a little, I sat under the lone little tree, for the first time tinged with defeat. If she really felt so strongly, was it worth going on? Stripped of its beauty, and the magnetism of Temujin, this was an eagle world, and they were natural killers. I knew this, but I imagined the bonds of our knowing each other could withstand my mistakes. And my error had surely been in not following the normal pattern of quiet movement. I had taken her by surprise, by straightaway running to the aerie; and this, to her, spelled uncertainty, not eagerness. She never had to be devious with me; she came in straight and true, not having to wonder if I spelled danger, knowing I did not.

She knew, quite well, that I would dodge to evade her, and knew just what my reactions would be and relied on them. She treated Arthur with respect, approached him with cunning when he was unprotected by his stick. As he always behaved the same, so did I. But this time my movements had been dictated without regard for her reaction and she chastised me thoroughly and deservedly.

Arthur pointed out sensibly that I was being femininely sentimental about a very unsentimental predator. "Why not just watch them without getting all involved?" he asked quietly.

But it was not that easy anymore. Each time I held up the food to her the impossibility of it seemed to recede a little. Maybe it was my imagination, but I felt the bond grow tighter, that she watched me with greater understanding. Now, I had spoiled the thread between us, and I was angry with myself. I knew, too, that I had taken enough punishment for one day.

The hide would have to wait. Today, she was in total charge, and I was not enthusiastic about proving her wrong. Arthur and Peter did not blame me. "Sorry, this day belongs to the eagles," I said, "I'm beat." And I started to pack up, the hide rolled up in my rucksack a mockery.

The gale roared its approval, slapping the eagles on their backs as they circled above me. As always, I was irresistibly lost in their grace and wonder. The certainty came seeping back that one day I would bridge the gap between us. One day the mother would come near enough to confirm that my regard for her was returned. One day, no matter how battered I now felt, she would see that the food I offered her was from a friend. But not today.

I was ready to go. I hefted my rucksack over my shoulders, and then I stopped. From the rock face above the sound of the wind came the shrill, impatient cheep of a hungry eaglet. Temujin! With his irritable complaint, the day expanded. How had I ever thought it was all impossible? Gladness rose in me and burst, taking with it all doubt and hurt. I turned back to base, ready for anything.

There he sat, fluffy and cuddly now that he had dried out,

squeaking his heart out in a long, unbroken wail. His mother had the rabbit and she would not be long in coming to him. Already her spirited defiance had evaporated and she watched me idly as I admired her heir.

The clouds are lightly curled
round their golden houses,
Girdled with the gleaming world . . .

TENNYSON

Later, Peter and I climbed along the base of the rock face, wanting to find the discarded egg. We bashed our way through curtains of bushes and thorny vines and found ourselves on a crazily uneven track used by mountain animals or sheep. Once or twice we surprised untidy old rams and admired their agility in negotiating the steep slopes. They looked like shaggy Rip Van Winkles.

Mocking chats kept up a lively commentary. Strange flowers hung from rocks. Water forced through to form small grottoes. Ferns and begonias were rife. Huge slabs lay around us, forming dark caves, and we wondered if, as one story told, they hid the entrances to tunnels far back into the mountain before rock falls sealed the openings.

Hyraxes bobbed up all around us, popping back into their homes among the rocks. Here I met the grandfather of them all. I had often noticed him as I sat on my ledge above the aerie, too large not to notice . . . a fat potentate surrounded by his wives, he lolled on his side on the warm rocks like an unlovely millionaire who did not have to worry, with all his wealth, about what people thought of his tummy or his habits. He lived immediately beneath the aerie and knew it would be difficult for the eagles to get a strike at him. So he lay in smug abandon among the boulders, complacent in his safety about being part of a family that is the eagles' staple diet.

Looking at him I could only marvel that he belongs to the same family as the elephant. In South Africa he is called a dassie or rock rabbit, a well-known, endearing small creature except when his population is unchecked. A vegetarian, he overruns sheep grazing areas. To many farmers, therefore, the presence of eagles in the vicinity does not spell loss of their lambs, but rather the control of hyrax numbers.

His feet are highly specialized for hanging on to rocks. The front ones have no claws in the four stubby toes, and the leathery pads, which are always damp, form suction caps. The hind feet have three toes ending in spatulate nails which, by turning the feet at an angle, he inserts into crevices for extra clinging power.

Search as we did, Peter and I found no sign of the egg.

We Begin to Be Part
of the Eagle World

Music bright as the soul of light,
for wings an eagle, for notes a dove . . .
                    SWINBURNE

The following week, Arthur was ahead of me and reached the gully well before I did. I could see him plodding up, very fit, looking around for the telltale spots in the sky. The mother must have been watching from beyond human vision for she dropped down so quickly that Arthur barely had time to duck and reach for a branch of a dead protea tree. I saw him going on, with the branch above his head, and I could hear her scream her disapproval of him. She let him get to base without further interest. Instead, she flew to and fro along the rock face, dipped down into the gully, her eyes and head searching from side to side. Then she rung up, higher and higher, and I knew it would be useless to sit still any longer. She had gone to have a good look around.

I reached the plateau and I could imagine her superb eyes missing nothing. She played with me, allowing me to almost reach the top before she deigned to acknowledge my existence.

I felt almost indignant that she could treat me with such majestic indifference. In this mood, I turned from the usual way along the

77

escarpment and made my way directly to the steep slopes of the summit. She was distinctly displeased by this retaliation since her known route of sweeping down on me over the bare escarpment became snarled up in unknown rocks and bushes that broke the rhythm of her flight.

From the summit I ran, ducked and dodged my way down to base. "Touché," I shouted as I slithered in against the rock. "Where did you get to?" demanded Arthur. "I could see her looking for you and was just on the point of going back to see what the two of you were up to." I was just ahead of the reproachful eagle and Arthur was forced to duck. "That's where I have been," I laughed. "She's been bullying me. She's bigger than I am." I watched her dawdling off, her fierce fun over for a time. And her aerial display was put on to remove any doubt that may have existed as to who were the owners of this mountain.

The gale blew against the rock face and, as it reached the immovable wall, deflected upward in a strong current. For us it meant a treacherous pull, and grit always in our eyes when we were near the edge, but the eagles reveled in it, using this invisible bank of power to hold them aloft. They held their wings rigid, the primaries spread wide and the tips upward, the white "windows" letting through the sun, while the tail, moving constantly, did all the steering and kept the balance. As soon as they hit the rock-face wind their wings clicked into place and the tails took over control.

Today the wind was rampant. The plain was like a suntrap and the warm air flooded up into thermals on which the eagles rolled or spiraled up, up out of sight.

At times Arthur and I were lifted almost bodily by the force of the wind. I held up the rabbit to her, then went over toward the slope above the aerie, where I usually placed it in readiness for Arthur's camera. "Of *course* she won't take it yet," I said, when Arthur shook his head, smiling, "but one day she will. It's time she understood that the rabbits come from *us*." No sooner had I put the rabbit on the slope than she winged in next to me, and lofted it away. I belayed Arthur down, then joined him.

What a difference a week had made! The nest was cleaner, there was no sign of the carcass that had covered the newborn Temujin. He sat in baby splendor, like a woolly toy. The protective sacs were

78

gone from his eyes. He might be a potential killer, but right now he was an enchanting small creature.

Confident that I had a little time in hand while his mother was away on the butcher's block, I made my tricky way along the ledge, picked him up and hugged him. He made no protest, and I leaned against the rock face holding in my arms the small body covered with springy, soft wool that would one day fly above me in eagle glory.

One day nothing would hold him from the freedom of the skies, but now he was close, content to be with me; and I loved him greatly.

He watched me making my way back along the edge. It was like leaving a pet. I whistled to him and he cocked his head on one side. I was behind the hessian when his mother winged over with part of the rabbit.

Arthur and I felt happy that the hide would allow us to be part of the aerie, but this was the mother's first experience of it and she was not quite sure about it.

We huddled in the confined space as she alighted, the food beneath her talons, and looked at the strange object on the ledge. Temujin cried impatiently and she fussed at him, but did not allow her heart to affect her cautious head. She waited, quite still. Occasionally she pounded the meat with her talons, but otherwise, except for her darting eyes, she did not move. We crouched, waiting.

For well over an hour we became colder and stiffer, realizing that any movement now would ever after connect the hide with suspicion. The falcons, oblivious of our proximity, whipped up and down past our weary eyes, their wings intimate with every quirk of the wind.

How long would she wait? The male eagle orbited above and she called to him. But he was difficult, remembering that she had not allowed him to have much to do with his son, or to feed him. He could see that she was set to ruin the boy and she could get on with it; no need to call on *him* when she was in trouble now. All the same, it was hard to ignore her pleas. Sometimes when she called it meant the wondrous togetherness in the sky. He was perplexed, though, wondering why she withheld the food from the wailing eaglet, until he noticed that she was absorbed with the strange object against the rock above the aerie.

Why did she hesitate? To him it did not present much problem. There was no sign of the humans. But if she wanted his masculine assurance—and it seemed she did—then he supposed he had better give it to her to keep the peace. He flew in to the aerie and defiantly bent over his son. But he retreated hastily when the eaglet, furious that his father's beak fondled his neck but brought no food, set up an awful, lusty squawking of baby reproach.

Left on her own again, the female still hesitated, not convinced.

The final seal of acceptance came from an unexpected quarter. A laughing dove, cooing contentedly, came ambling along the ledge. Reaching the high pile of sticks, it looked up and saw the fearsome picture before it. It was quite undismayed. The eagle watched it speculatively, its eyes flitting backward and forward from the dove to the hide. Nothing happened. The little dove unconcernedly stretched out one colorful wing down its leg, letting each feather have a turn of the sun. Still nothing happened. It nodded its head in the soporific warmth of the little suntrap it had found, and the eagle bent over to get a better view, her dark eyes still flickering from hide to the dozing dove. And still nothing leaped out from the object above her to pounce on it. The scene was so filled with peace that the eagle had no further doubts, and was completely satisfied.

The mother began to shred the meat from the carcass and to nudge it gently into Temujin's mouth, effectively muffling his irritable squeaking. Once embarked on the absorbing task of seeing that he got the correct proportions of liver and heart, bone and fur, she paid the hide no further attention, even when it was obvious that she could hear the sound of the camera. Temujin's throat labored to swallow the chunks, but a steady stream of saliva from his mother's beak eased them down. He didn't gape all the time, as did other baby birds, but waited until the food was thrust against his beak. He was soon a very full little eagle. His crying changed to throaty grunts of contentment, as though he were burping.

Gone now were the stiffness and soreness I had felt, gone with the picture unfolding before me, the metamorphosis of a roaring jet of savagery into this soft, gentle mother feeding her offspring.

The Saturdays stretched out. I spent weekends in the lee of the mountain, curled in a sleeping bag. I wakened to the sharp crack of icicles breaking inches from my face. I lay in the wonder of stars so near and bright in the mountain air that I could almost touch them. I looked at the dawn and the gradual awareness of eagles watching me gravely while I cracked the ice over a small pool in the rocks. I looked out on an eagle world, vast, lonely, but very beautiful.

Arthur's camera began to record the story as, one by one, the days unfolded the love, drama, ferocity, tension, humor and heartache; the breathtaking beauty and the harshness of the elements, there on that rock face, while a small eagle burst from its shell and grew to soar in the South African sky above the Drakensberg.

.

The Day of the Kite

Over the land it sailed, collecting height,
Flapped in the face of each offended crow . . .
CAMPBELL

At two weeks, Temujin's woolly covering was a paler, yellowish color compared with the previous off-white. He looked like a plump duckling. His eyes were wide open and showed keen interest in any movement around him. When his mother looked toward the hide, so did he. If he saw us on the ledge while his mother was away, he watched us intently, or ignored us, as the mood took him. He turned at my whistle, cried incessantly the cry of a wound-up toy, for it neither really complained nor did it reach any high peaks of distress. It just went on and on. His beak and talons were growing and were not the soft things they had been before, and their color was starting to change to a beige. The hook was beginning to emerge from his beak.

We had gone down to the hide straightaway because the wind was ominously absent. From the gully I had had to watch the mother all the way and, on occasions, I had been glad of my rucksack, the only protection between my back and her talons.

But once we were behind the hide, she turned on all the joy she brought as we watched her feeding Temujin, and ignoring us.

Remembering her frisking of me, I told myself many things: "I think she'd like to like me, that she does, in fact, but she has to put on this big act. You know, when people are afraid of being demonstrative in their love or affection, afraid of being caught out in a show of tenderness."

Arthur shook his head. "She would rip you at the drop of a hat, and probably will, if you go getting sentimental about her." But I knew that she and I could be friends in a wild if remote sort of way.

Arthur seemed to prove his own theory as I belayed him to the hide. Exposed to her attentions, I shouted up at her in mock anger: "Just when I am giving you a buildup, you silly old lady, you go and spoil the whole thing." Unconcernedly, her activity over for a while, she flew off and sat nonchalantly on her favorite rock. "You see," I said to Arthur as I slid down to the hide, "there she sits quite peacefully, liking me." Arthur snorted. "You are kidding yourself," he returned. "She is just tired."

Respite from the wind was short-lived; and Temujin was obviously hungry. So I agreed to return to base and provide Temujin's lunch. But I had planned without thought of his mother. The wind slashed me against the rock, and the female eagle took delight in trying to shove me off. She used no talons; knowing she had me cornered, she just sat on the summit. Every time I made a move, she shot down over me in express flight. I was trapped like a moth on a pin.

Arthur saw my predicament, not able to help. But after a while he shouted, "I'll give them one of the pigeons I brought with me. I was curious to see if they would be interested in eating them. I don't think they will," he said, "but it may distract the female's attention from you."

He aimed, and threw one of the dead pigeons onto the edge of the aerie. We had never ever seen the eagles attack any other birds, although we knew they ate guinea fowls, so we were dubious. And then fascinated. For Temujin became highly excited at the strange food on his nest. He had no idea what it was, what to do with it, but you would have thought he had invented it. He called shrilly to his mother and thrust his small beak in amongst the feathers. She came in, all indignant parent, chastising her son for accepting gifts from strangers. It perplexed her, that much was obvious; and it was alien, that much she knew. Pigeons did not just die on an eagle's aerie like that.

I became so captivated with the happenings down there that I forgot the purpose of the exercise—to give me a chance to get back to base. Arthur had a grandstand view and made the most of it, but even though I realized the air above me was now free of eagles, I did not make for safety, for suddenly the mother eagle, with a great deal of fuss, distastefully grabbed the pigeon and shot up into the air with it. I was astonished, not believing that she meant to eat it. She didn't! She played with it!

Spiraled on the bank of wind until to a fair height, she opened her talons and the pigeon started its tumble. With a breathtaking swoop, she was on to it, catching it, then letting it go so low that we held our breath thinking she had lost it, at the last moment to grab it casually with one foot and thrust it upward. The male joined her.

Rising above him, she dropped the pigeon down on him. He swerved and dived after it, joining in the game. Now she made him do the fetching. Cottoning on to it, he went off in a huff and she became bored with the whole thing. Turning her back on the pigeon, she chased her mate. Together, they arrowed to the clouds, delighting in each other.

"O.K.," came the practical voice from the ledge, "show's over. Now what about that rabbit." Rabbits, complete with fur, were hard to come by, and I was always full of respect for Arthur's ingenuity in raising them. When he managed to locate one he added it to the small reserve in the family's Deepfreeze. "One day I'll recommend you for an award—the best rabbit finder for eagles," I promised. "Where did *this* come from?"

"From a nun who breeds rabbits for her orphanage," he replied.

I imagined him pleading his cause. For how could she possibly believe that he was willing to pay top price for a dead rabbit to feed an eaglet whose parents would, in turn, try to rip us to pieces as we tendered our gift? Food was scarce, he probably told her. And no doubt, she offered him a blank face, took the money and said she'd pray for him.

Deep-frozen rabbits, we found, became very soft as the ice melted. Their skin was so thin that it was inclined to disintegrate. We kept the carcass firm by trying nylon line to the feet, winding it round the body and then attaching a piece of catapult elastic, so that the whole rabbit could hang from a rucksack, our rucksacks being so full that this was the only thing we could do.

Now, seeing there was no sign of the eagles for the moment, I walked to the edge, beginning to unwind the nylon. "Do me a favor while you can," shouted Arthur, "and throw me down my anorak." Before dashing to base I looped the elastic round the piton that secured Arthur's belaying rope, as a safeguard against the wind blowing it over the edge.

Then, out of the blue, the eagle plunged. As usual, I was bewitched by the beauty of her, but, apart from this, my coordination is not always razor sharp; I get there, but not particularly quickly. So it was that she was away ahead of me. She was on her way before I realized this time she was not after me, but the rabbit. She was about to be a clear winner, too, I could see, but I determined to have some say in the proceedings since I knew Arthur would be fed up if the rabbit went now. She fell on it as I ran over, slithering along the edge, throwing a shower of small stones over Arthur as I skidded to a stop. "What's going on?" he shouted. The next minute he knew.

The eagle clutched the rabbit. The nylon stretched to its limit. The eagle felt the drag of the elastic and suddenly let the rabbit go. It flung straight back and caught me in the shoulder, bounced over the edge, and thumped on the rock face. Overwhelmed by the unexpectedness of it all, I still managed to make for the nylon and began hauling it in so that I could get the weight off it and disentangle it from the piton.

Now both eagles dived at the rabbit. Arthur had to lean back into the rock to avoid the astonishing melee. The female clutched it just as I had pulled it up to the edge and the line went taut again. I could do little else but hang on, with the nylon line wound round my hands. The rabbit was gripped in talons of steel, the line cut into my palms. For some minutes we stayed like that. Then slowly, surely I was being drawn toward the cliff drop. Sharp pebbles cut through my jeans and sometimes I was airborne as gusts of wind gave the eagle the advantage.

In a lull of the gale I made the mistake of relaxing a little.

I was jerked upright. The eagle spread over me like a great black kite riding the wind.

The day of the kites, I thought incongruously! I had always been fascinated with tales of the Tibetans who on propitious days flew their kites in the Himalayas, watched over by a Kite Master. Man-size box kites, eight or nine feet square and ten feet long, with great, wide wings, kites large enough to hold a monk. The kite ropes had to be held by horses or a crowd of people as the wind tugged them to the Gods of the Air.

These kites carried messages written on silk, prayers destined for the eternal heights where the Wind God unfurled the silk and read the prayers of the monks for safety against danger. Sometimes the kites did not become properly airborne or the "pilot" was not adept at navigating. Then the monk could be seen vainly trying to keep his balance in the crazily wobbling craft as it ducked and dived; or, sometimes, lost his last finger grip and turned over and over as he fell to his death thousands of feet below.

I thrust down further thought of these macabre endings and silently sent my own request humming up the nylon for the eagle kite to take to the Gods of the Wind: "Let him live, O Gods, this baby Temujin, and his parents with him. And let him grow into a great South African black eagle, proud, strong and free."

The eagle had won. I slid to the precipice and, at the last moment, had to let go. My eagle kite leaped up at the release of pressure and I heard the sharp crack of the nylon as it broke against the piton.

She looked back fleetingly at me, the look of a victor. But I was far from cowed. I exulted in the courage of her. The thread, tangible this time, swung between us. Would she have taken the chance with anyone she feared or hated?

I looked at her trailing the nylon line while her mate followed nervously, without much of a backward thought for me. But I know that part of me winged its way with them, carrying my thanks to the Gods of the Wind.

Hats Off!

He that hath no head needs no hat . . .
ENGLISH PROVERB

It was a day for precision flying and bitterly cold. But the sun is never far away in South Africa. I normally wore a tartan cloth hat to shade my eyes.

On this day, when Temujin was three weeks old, I had changed the hat for a woolen cap, the sort worn by the Zulus and the Basotho, pulled over my ears. It was a day the eagles loved, favoring swift dives, and I wondered how I was going to fare on my own when I belayed Arthur to the hide. We could only wait for the wind to drop.

Peter and I sat against our rock at base as the wind kicked at the mountain and tugged at unwilling clouds. Peter recorded the gale and the shouts of the eagles while I watched my family of field mice eating their breakfast.

I had befriended them the previous year, inviting them with bread. They came to within a couple of feet of me, picked up the food in their two front feet, then washed their faces and whiskers.

They were great entertainment on days like this when the wind was too strong to approach the precipice. Capering about with their babies, all golden and cute, they would climb into my rucksack pockets to ferret about in my lunch, and I had to make sure not to carry them off.

Sometimes, with snow all around the base, it was like a small world apart, full of Nature's delights. Large black ants laboriously built a fortress against an enemy that never seemed to arrive. Dung beetles, shiningly handsome in their brown-lustered armor, rolled droppings backward and forward to perfect the large ball they pushed about with the aid of their stout horn. A chameleon, knocked insensible and black with the frost, clung to a branch like a miniature brontosaurus until we retrieved it from the frozen shadows to give it the warmth of the sun, when it turned from the color of death to golden, living green. One day we watched a mole push out its blinded head, feel the blazing sun, then duck back into the dark underground again. How had it gotten all the way to the top of a high mountain?

Behind us, in the rock, was a colony of highly colored lizards that melted their rainbow bodies into the crevices, the only indication of their presence being the throbbing of a pulse in their tiny throats. They, too, soon unconcernedly sunned themselves, showing friendship by ignoring us. The base became more than a refuge against possible eagle talons. It was alive with small, beating wings and busy, scuttling feet, an island of life in vast wastes of snow and cold rock. Above it, like meteors, were the radiant wings of briefly visiting sunbirds, and high above, the spread of eagles.

As Peter did not come with us every week he did not know the moods of the eagles and the wind as well as Arthur and I. We had learned ways of protecting ourselves. We found also that the presence of three people was often inclined to confuse the female eagle and throw her out of predictable action. Peter sometimes went down to the hide and this was fine, for then the eagle could only see me at the top where I was director of the actress eagle and prop setting! Often he elected to stay on the plain, from where he had a grandstand view of dashing eagles and humans, and one of the greatest contributions this schoolboy gave, besides the recordings, was his capacity for finding enjoyment in the wild relationship between the female eagle and me. It was fun to have Peter there. He was quite sure I could look after myself and he knew what I thought about my eagles. His chuckles or infectious grins changed many a near-danger into a smiling near-miss. He quickly became a fine photographer, especially at action shots.

The only time I used a rope round my waist was when I went along the narrow ledge to see Temujin. At other times I slid down to the hide and hauled myself up on the rope tied to the piton at the top. Arthur worried about the safety of my sitting on my own at the top. Today, something seemed to be provoking the eagle. She was excitedly tense as she dived at me.

"I don't think she likes your cap," Arthur said.

"The hell with it," I exploded. "Next she'll be letting me know what to wear and what she likes for dinner."

The updraught from the rock face was frightening and Arthur, with his camera and rucksack to carry, had to fight strongly to get down.

"When I'm down," he shouted, "let her have the rabbit. You'll never stand against this wind, so throw it over toward the slope so I can get some flying sequences as she hangs over it before grab-bing."

I hunched behind the rucksacks and felt the currents of air lashing round my head as she flashed over and over. Whenever she came for a strike at me she gave a distinctive sort of whistle, unlike any of her other calls. She did it immediately above me. I had no time for any protective action—if action were possible—physically involved as I was with the rope, and mentally with the thought of the drop below Arthur.

At last he was down on the ledge and I secured the rope to the piton as the eagle flew over me. I saw her, from the corner of my eye, in front of me as I reached for the rabbit under the rucksack. In a second she was back, and woof! My head felt as though it had been hacked off. The biting wind tore at me. I gasped with the sensation of being scalped, and looked up.

She held my cap in one foot, looking down at the lightness of it. I laughed aloud as she showed her disgust by opening talons and letting the cap float down to the plain. I burst in merri-ment. "Arthur," I yelled, "she's taken my cap." And back came a matter-of-fact voice, "Never mind the cap, I'm waiting for the rab-bit."

I was furious, cold, battered and stunned, and the hunting eagle was coming back looking blue murder, anger in her. What good was a woolen cap to a family of eagles?

"Don't blame me," I shouted, "I could have told you it was no rabbit, but you took it without asking." She folded her wings and plunged again. Her talons flicked at me. "Arthur," I cried desperately. "My head!" His voice came through the whistling wind, "Never mind your head. I'm waiting for the rabbit."

I had had enough. I flung the rabbit to the slope. As far as I was concerned, everything and everyone could go to blazes. She came over, circling, calling. But she did not take the food. I was unnerved, angry, and I know I looked it, but she wove her spell, and, as always, I was undone watching her.

At her most appalling best, all ferocity and invincible wildness, she had the capacity to make me believe that she actually thought about things, that there did pass between us a definite message. I had no right to think this, but I did. She had given me the worst pasting I'd had, and she could have come straight in knowing I jibbed, knowing I was beaten. The way to the food was wide open. Endearingly, she had withheld the last punch, my whole attitude telling her she'd won, and that I was running away. I felt foolishly near to tears. But I knew with a warmth in my heart that *something* reached out to catch us in an intangible noose of understanding. We two women were in truth sorting *something* out on that mountain.

I crawled over to the edge, not caring whether she ripped me to bits. I could hear her calling as though trying to make me understand something, and I expected to feel the blow. But she did nothing, and after a while hurtled in for the food.

"Are you O.K.?" Arthur asked as I lay on the ledge. "O sure," I said quite calmly, camouflaging the pounding sense of discovery. "I'm without a head, but I'm going to stay here forever, here on this ledge." "You do that," replied Arthur. "We'll bring you food each week." Above the wind from base came Peter's amused laugh.

Now I looked at Temujin, all of three weeks old. He watched the shadows in the sky, his eyes bright. He had a distinct personality and, after he'd shown irritation a few times when his mother came into the nest without food, he had a few nudges of discipline from her. The father was on the butcher's block cleaning up the rabbit and the mother, impatient, cruised between him and the nest.

"Where's my cap?" I shouted at her. "She knows you sure enough," Arthur said. "She knows it's you, knows your voice, and she looks for you. Wonder what she thinks about you." "Probably that I'm crazy," I answered.

Soon she came in with part of the rabbit. Temujin wobbled to his feet and made a grab for it, until his legs collapsed and he keeled over.

His mother waited patiently knowing that he couldn't tear the meat yet. She waited lovingly and then began to push pieces of meat into his beak. He was fed the heart, the liver, and the very tender parts of muscle. He was still soft and cuddly and I wondered again how this little fat fellow would ever be able to wing in glory across the sky; wondered, too, how his mother, crumpling with soft devotion, could be the same giant whose beak could rip through skin and fur with one swift slash, and who, such a short time ago, had nearly knocked me unconscious as she took the cap from my head. How could I love her? How could I not, when I saw her like this with Temujin?

Hungry no more, he lay next to the fur of the carcass, sleepy and content. I whistled down to him and he lazily turned in the direction of the sound. "Someone up here loves you," I sang out. But he didn't seem to think it very important.

Learning to Know
the Wind

The wind bloweth where it listeth,
and thou hearest the sound thereof,
but canst not tell when it cometh,
and either it goeth . . .

ST. JOHN

We only had one regular day a week in which to put the wonder of these rare predators on film. Time was against us, the weather, and the wind. In three months Temujin would leave the aerie. He would soon be flying and they would all move farther afield.

As I had learned to "read the wind" and so, most times, evade eagle talons, we gradually worked out ways and means for Arthur's filming. I was the focus of the female's rough attentions. She knew me and was prepared to bargain with me, so we used two phrases which, each time employed, unconsciously drew us together.

One was to "bring her in." The other, from Arthur, "You two women had better sort things out . . ."

Both were dependent on the wind.

There were winds for flying, winds for flying as little as possible. The former gave us days filled with eagles in the sky, eagles on the aerie, eagles on the move. The wind always blew around the mountain, but sometimes it was a Berg wind, warm and dry, and the lassitude it produced in us was also apparent in the eagles.

On these days they did not feel like arguing too long. After warning us in the gully they sat on their favorite rocks for long spells at a time. The only way to get them mobile again was to stand on the escarpment and look down at the aerie. This immediately made the female airborne, coming to see what I was doing.

Often I went over toward them as they stood midway between the aerie and the butcher's block, calling to her, swinging the rabbit. Eventually I could approach to within a few yards before the male flew off, then much closer until the female called out as if pleading with me not to ask her to make the final contact.

We stayed companionably on our separate rocks, but when I started back to the aerie with the rabbit, she was total huntress, chasing me all the way. When I had thus "brought her in," I got the rabbit ready for Arthur's photography, and gave him a running commentary of the eagle's flight and direction. After a time this team effort was so perfected that it seldom failed.

"Circling," I'd shout, "lower . . . no, top of the mountain now . . . circling again . . . she's gone off . . . relax . . . Coming back! Getting ready! Okay, looks likely . . . dropping a little, but still near the summit . . . okay! Coming in! Wings hunched! Talons away . . . Coming in . . . in . . . nearer . . . nearer . . . nearer . . . nearer . . . NOW!"

My voice would rise to a crescendo and she would be over the edge. And Arthur, on the ledge below, assessing all my jumbled information like a computer, would know exactly when to press the shutter. I was never quite sure, right up to the last second, whether the eagle's puckish humor would prompt her to have a go at me instead of the rabbit.

And Arthur was never certain whether he would get a rabbit, an eagle, a spray of stones, or me in his camera lens!

But his pictures, his filming of these dual efforts were unbelievable, the eagle caught, head angled with purpose, talons surely round the food, at precisely the right second.

The two women "sorting it out" was a purely feminine affair which Arthur accepted. I began to realize that I knew this lovable old battler very well indeed. Without thinking too deeply, I could tell what mood she was in, whether it would be best for flight photography, shots on the nest, or strike pictures. We had come a long way, this eagle and I. We accepted each other in the light of our respective worlds, and she could no more make me instinctively aggressive to her than I could tame her to human subservience. Once we had sorted this out I loved her capacity to remain utterly wild, yet knowing she could trust me. She no longer minded our being there on the mountain. And this was something very heartwarming.

Some days, when it was cold and wet, she held her right leg against her as though the old wound pained her or she suffered from rheumatism or arthritis. Then it was awful to watch her suffering. On one dreadful day when we arrived, her head was slashed and bleeding. Unthinking, I ran toward her, wanting to give her sympathy. I felt futile, unable to help as she cawed in bedraggled melancholy.

On these days when Arthur said, "You two women . . . ," all I wanted to do was to see that she did not have to hunt with her painful foot, that she had peace and quiet. I said "hello" to Temujin, left the food near his forlorn mother, and we went quietly away.

The Prize

Not all that tempts your wand'ring eyes
And heedless hearts, is lawful prize;
Nor all that glisters, gold . . .
                    THOMAS GRAY

When Temujin was a month old we took a guinea fowl in place of a rabbit. The food we took the eaglet was always eagerly taken by his parents, and so that we would all get the best out of it, we used it briefly as a lure for the camera.

The day was misty, shrouded in a moving grayness. At the gully the eagle dropped weirdly from the unknown beyond the mist, but, strangely, there was no further evidence of her presence, even after I had belayed Arthur to the hide.

"There she is," he called, pointing to the black form cruising around. The clammy mist seemed to be effecting us all, eagle and human, into withdrawm silence.

Because of the quiet, I moved round to an outcrop slab in the escarpment, in view of the aerie and of Arthur on his ledge, and began to tape Temujin's voice while the coast seemed clear and peaceful. I kept the circling eagle form constantly in sight as it veered in and out of the mist. When it moved to the summit and started to fly backward and forward across it, I turned my face toward it, my back toward the sheer drop below. The wind was

99

steady with no treacherous gusts, so I was quite safe as long as I kept the eagle in view. The tape recorder turned.

"Watch it," screamed Arthur, his voice a thunderclap.

Suddenly, I was flung against the back of the ledge where I stood, all breath gone, and bounced back. I had just managed to get a hand to the rock above me and haul up the leg that hung over the edge of the escarpment, when I heard Arthur again, his voice rising to a bellow. "For God's sake look *out!*"

The emphasis on the last word coincided with a second thump on my back. I didn't wait for anything else. I started running for base. I could feel the lunging body behind me and flung myself into a large crack that cut back into the escarpment. I felt the grip of my nylon sweater as a sharp talon caught it at the waist and tore it up to my neck. Again she tore, this time hitting flesh, and now I knew I had only the time it would take her to complete the arc of her flight before she was back again. Base seemed a lifetime away!

It was all my fault! I had been watching the male! He'd never been quite so close in before but had obviously been left in charge and, in the deception of the mist, I had made my mistake. I could well imagine the female returning and being unable to resist the temptation of my inviting back, a sitting duck of a human, not remembering her vigilance.

Even young Peter, in the shelter of base, leaped up in concern. It was he who washed my raked back with the only liquid on the hard, dry mountain . . . a lone can of beer I kept tucked away in my rucksack.

That made it two strikes to the eagle, but I was by no means routed. The day was not yet over. The sun began to rise and my spirits with it. By the time the mist dispersed, I was ready to show my eagle friend that I hadn't given up. To show her that I held nothing against her I stuck the guinea fowl in a forked stick and waved it in the air. She came over, interested in what I was doing. Then, seeing the stick at closer quarters, she became passionately angry.

"Sorry," I said quickly, realizing suddenly the cause of her wrath, "I honestly forgot."

It was the first time I had ever wielded a stick even connected with food, and she was beside herself with outrage. I was impressed with this vivid display. *She* was allowed to take me by surprise, bash me about, put scratches down my back, hunt me out of holes. But *I* was pleased to remember the rules. Her rules. On no account were there to be sticks from me.

Arthur and I were amicably arguing about whether, with my torn back, I felt like belaying him to the ledge again. I was quite happy to do it and went toward the ropes, pu ting the "sticked" guinea fowl on the edge. After the morning's events I should have been prepared for anything, but again she took me completely by surprise. While I stood waiting, she tore down and snatched up the guinea fowl, stick and all. In studied effrontery, she had taken our precious "prop," which had, as yet, done no work for us.

I was abashed. Arthur was livid. The eagle was triumphant. But not for long.

"Look!" shouted Peter.

Arthur and I ducked. But the eagle was not coming in at us. A martial eagle had made a grab for the guinea fowl and the black eagle was streaking away from it to the summit. There the two giants rolled and swerved, talons contesting for the guinea fowl.

"What now?" Arthur shouted as I started moving toward them. "That guinea fowl's ours," I flung over my shoulder, "and I'm going to get it." He didn't say what I knew he thought!

The two eagles locked talons, twisted and turned like a corkscrew. They disappeared behind the rocks, then up they shot, there to fight it out, the guinea fowl forgotten. By the time I reached the arena, they had disappeared in feathered confusion over the other side of the mountain. I staggered toward the remains of the prey. As I did so, two shadows raced across the rough grass, dived at the carcass, at each other and at me. Then a third shadow came and two more, as the male eagle and a pair of buzzards leaped into the fray. The guinea fowl was tossed around like a rugby ball. The only way I could be sure where it fell was by their concerted lunges at it. I could hear Arthur from a long ways away, shouting it did not matter. But I could be tenacious, too. It was my fault that the guinea fowl "prop" had gone. They could have it after it had done its work.

I grabbed at it a second before the female eagle. Over thirty-five feet of combined wingspans spun about my head in a melee of cutting primaries and moving wings. Five pairs of clicking, slashing talons clashed. Having lost sight of the prey, they turned on each other. Only later did the black eagles manage to get rid of the usurpers. I held up the battered trophy.

"As a prop player I'm not so good," I said, "but here is your photographic guinea fowl. I won it, but only just."

Peter was highly diverted and I realized that I must have cut a very comical picture.

I wondered, later, if the mother eagle recognized the object which had caused all the fuss, when she winged in to take it to Temujin. It had been worth an argument. Arthur's pictures were pure gold.

The month-old eaglet was ravenous. Food was scarce.

Temujin had lost the baby darkness of his eyes. Now they were flecked with light, the hoods over them much more pronounced. His talons were enormous and quite the most prominent part of him. Along his wingtips was the first sign of feathers—a thin black line showing the start of the primaries. His whole body was latent with growth. Under the springy wool things were beginning to happen quickly, waiting to burst through. He wobbled to his feet as his mother came with the guinea fowl.

Propping himself on his outstretched wings, he tried to tug at the meat. He was so hungry that she fed him straightaway. Although he managed to extract one or two shreds, to his vast delight he was more than content to let his mother do he work. Finally he shook his head in tired negation when his mother tried to force more food down his throat, moving it from side to side to dodge her beak. He could hardly stir, but she reminded him of his manners and nudged him to a standing position. He shuffled on the aerie and positioned his woolly bottom over the edge. He had graduated!

Till now, to keep the nest clean, he had backed toward the rock face, unsure of his balance. Now he was a big boy. He wobbled up and down, sitting precariously over the sheer drop, his talons clutching the branches. Growing up had many requirements, but this was not one of them.

A Ring and a Spy

Sent to spy out the land . . .
NUMBERS

Thunderheads piled against the heavens. The wind pushed the day along, chivying flaky clouds like a teacher with her charges at a Sunday school picnic. Though the sun was all about us, we could see lightning splintering the far horizon. I wondered what this new day would bring.

Arthur had previously mentioned "ringing" the eaglet but I had thought little about it. Now he said, "It would be great if you could do it."

He held an aluminum ring bearing the legend, NOTIFY PRETORIA ZOO, SOUTH AFRICA. 658.007. Little Temujin in the 007 tradition! A small James Bond, licensed to kill!

My thoughts about ringing birds were far from crystallized, and only in terms of pigeons and small birds. I was not quite sure whether I agreed with it. The pros and the cons I knew. And, whatever we did, as with the whole eagle story, there would be critics!

I remember watching a bird man ringing wild birds near my village. He had caught a European swallow in a mist net, and was carefully recording details of the bird and the ring. "Think of how much we have learned about these wonderful little migrants," he

103

said, "and most of it from rings." He told me about the storehouse of knowledge being compiled from the history of bird rings. How else would I know about the amazing journey of the swallows—over six thousand miles to South Africa, and another six thousand miles back to Britain again each year? How else would it be proved that, returning to England to nest, they go to the same area, often to the same house and same nest, for as long as they survive the awesome flight? I believed the bird man, but I confess that the idea was less appealing when it involved the eagle wings and talons cutting down on me.

I felt the light ring. "Best not to handle it too much," Arthur advised. "It is soft and malleable, but the more it is rubbed and worked, the harder and firmer it becomes. You will get it on easily, and Temujin will do the rest."

Despite the sun the cold was like steel as it flung round the mountain, razoring my ears and cutting at my eyes. I pulled my Zulu cap over my ears and prepared to face the gully.

"It's that cap again," Arthur said, "she really does prefer your hat." He had been watching the eagle bombard me for some time and had reached this pithy conclusion. I was exasperated, finding it difficult to believe that an eagle could have such an aversion to such a human thing as a cap. But I took it off. And she seemed mollified.

When we reached our base I put it on again, partly because my head was becoming numb and partly to challenge her to prove her dislike of it. She roared in, did a quick turn and continued her attack. There was absolutely no doubt about it—my cap was complete anathema to her. Arthur was highly amused. "Why don't you give it to her," he suggested. "What she thinks looks terrible on you she may think will suit her down to the ground."

I had a feeling the conversation was getting a little out of hand and that Arthur would very much like to film the eagle taking the cap off my head as she had done previously. I threw the offending cap down and she whipped over it without a moment's hesitation. "Hey!" Arthur shouted, "give me time!"

She charged, propelling past me, and bore the offending headgear away. I thought this was stretching friendship too far, especially as I never recovered it, although being sentimental about favorite things, Peter and I searched for it all over the mountain.

She returned after a while and I, still conscious of the nearness of her, went over to the slope and held up the rabbit. She veered in, then sped flippantly away. "Forget it," Arthur said, "there's no chance." Not today, perhaps, I thought, but one day she'll come right in. As each day went by I believed it more.

"Let's give her the rabbit straightaway," I said suddenly, "then go down and ring the prince."

I swung the rabbit aloft again, and again she circled nearer. The moment held before she swung away. "You are certainly a trier," Arthur smiled as I threw the rabbit on the turf, conceding defeat for this time, "but no eagle will come in that close." I stood and waited.

But this was to be ladies' day! Before he had time to finish speaking, she rocketed in. Slashing my leg with her wing, she fell on the rabbit and lifted it into the air. I was keenly aware of the sound of wind-whipped feathers and the thump of taloned feet right next to me. The picture of her closeness stayed with me long after she had gone. I stood there, alone with the token of her confidence, her message that said so clearly that she knew me.

"Come on," Arthur said, "we don't have much time." If she followed her usual pattern, she would be on the butcher's block only the short time it took to rip the rabbit and bring the headless carcass to Temujin. No, we did not have much time.

Peter was on my ledge ready to shout a warning. Arthur was on the hide. Everyone was accounted for. The male flew aimlessly above. I was edging along to the aerie with my back to the rock face so that I could anticipate the approach of the eagles against the sun if they returned before I had finished the ringing.

. . . What dangers thou canst make us scorn! . . .

BURNS

I picked Temujin up and extricated his leg, knowing I had to do the job quickly and calmly if I was to avoid the drop below and the possible onslaught of an eagle. I whistled quietly to him and murmured endearing things. Temujin had known both sounds since he was born and was quite unconcerned. I pressed the ring firmly into the springy wool, placed it so that when the wool turned into trouser feathers it would drop naturally into place above his "wrist." I hugged him, holding him close. "Soon," I said, "soon, my

105

little rider of heaven." His talons clung to me as I leaned over to return him to the aerie.

Arthur had his eye to his camera, thinking as I did that we had time in hand. Peter was absorbed in the happenings below him. I was hating leaving Temujin. So we all missed the lethal black body until she reached us.

She shouted, Arthur bellowed. The noise stayed her slating for a moment. She skirted past the overhang above the aerie again and again. As I crouched against the side, her wingtips cut across my back. Only Arthur's voice stopped her. His shout seemed to freeze her talons to last-minute inaction, and I was extremely grateful for it.

I had hoped to do the ringing without the eagle's knowledge. I hated to show that we meant danger to her chick. But I had reckoned on time alone. I had overlooked eagle wisdom.

Temujin was obviously puzzled by his parents' relentless attack on me. Even his father was coming in very close. Each time they passed the nest the eaglet ducked with me, his head close to mine. At least he is for me, I thought, as a talon probed my shoulder and Temujin shied back against the rock.

"After I have gone," I told him, "tell them I meant you no harm."

"Okay," Arthur said in a hoarse voice, very concerned, "you've got a chance now."

I was defenseless, but it was now or never. They would not be gone for long. Temujin turned his frowning eyes to mine as I left him to make my way back to the hide, and he stretched out his neck to watch me. He lowered his head before his mother lunged at me, aware of her before I was. As her wings crossed my bottom, Arthur hauled me up over the hide ledge.

How had she known? We had always been sure of her being away much longer on the butcher's block after we had given her the rabbit. This time she had returned almost straightaway, and without the food.

"He's the spy," I said suddenly, pointing to the male flying unobtrusively above us, "he is more 'clued up' than we give him credit for."

Out of sight of the butcher's block, the female could not have known that we meant to do anything different from other days. But her mate had seen me making for the aerie and, while he was not prepared to tackle me, he could at least instigate the charge. So he had told her. We looked at him with new respect.

After the holocaust I watched Temujin quietly from the hide. His pin feathers, at five weeks, were through, and there were feather tufts in the wool on his wingtips. His tail was beginning to take definite form. The eagle shape of him was there, under the clinging baby fluff, waiting for the right moment to emerge in its entirety. His beak, which would always tear but never peck, was strengthening into hard bone, and he was soon showing its worth as he tore at the rabbit brought in by his mother, now that things were back to normal.

I was worried about her, wondering if she intended coming in as usual after what she might think was a betrayal. She was made of enduring stuff, this old defender. Hazard lived with her. She looked truculently at the hide as she pounded the rabbit down, looked at Temujin, found both satisfactory, and took off into the wind. Her son was safe. We were out of sight and, for the present, out of mind as she called to her mate and raced for the clouds. She had had enough excitement, earthly excitement, for one day.

Flames Over the Mountain

And after the fire a still small voice . . .
KINGS

How long would Temujin live?

I remember reading about eagles when I was small, in Arthur Mee's *Children's Encyclopaedia:*

"It takes an elephant a long time to grow up, and it takes him a long time to wear out. Well treated, he should live to be a hundred. That is the age to which an eagle is supposed to live, but some people put down the age he may reach as 200 years. Even that is young compared with the life of a whale. This can be shown to last for 500 years. Indeed, some whales that have been caught are believed to be 1,000 years old."

Present-day ornithologists tend to stick to the conservative forty- to fifty-year life-span of an eagle. That is the answer I get when I question people. I believe that, like Arthur Mee's elephant, a black eagle takes a long time to grow up—four years to maturity—and that it will not "wear out" after only a comparatively short life-span.

Temujin was not yet two months, whatever life-span was in store for him and whatever hazards he had to face. And there would be many, I thought, as I trudged up the mountain toward him.

A misty drizzle vied with the sun. Long, curved grass stalks held moving lines of glistening drops. The ground was sodden. I concentrated on finding footholds and paid little attention to the shrouded heights until we reached the plain.

The mountain reared before me, an insensate mass of blackened earth pitted with stark boulders. Damp grass zigzagged with lines of spluttering flame stopped only by pockets of snow. Bushes at the base of the rock face smoldered, smoke furled upward. Everywhere was utter desolation. Whirlwinds of burned grass cartwheeled into the mist, and falling rocks bounced in a flurry of cindered dust. There was no sign of life. No flap-flap of rock pigeons' wings or mournful sound of doves, no movement of hyraxes among the rocks. Suddenly I picked out a pair of falcons spinning in the smoke, and a sunbird flitted against the black earth.

Veld fires are a common feature of South Africa's winter landscapes, in which grass is burned to promote fresh growth with the arrival of spring rains. But a mountain fire is more rare here in the Drakensberg than in the Cape. Sometimes the sides of Table Mountain are charred black with driving flame. In any locality they are an awesome sight.

We stared in the direction of the rock face, trying to see beyond the smoke. No, I thought! In my imagination I saw the fire roaring by me to reach the dry sticks of the aerie. "No. Please God, no!" I murmured.

Arthur, visibly upset, would want to prepare for every eventuality; I did not want the possibility of it put into words. I started running. This was the Mountain of the Gods, and this the year of the eagles. And had not my message and prayer gone up to those Gods on the wings of a kite?

My feet crunched on the blistered earth and my breath fought with my throat.

"Stop!" Arthur shouted. I shook my head. "Stop," he called. And I heard the beginning of gladness in his voice.

I looked up. She rose, trailing veils of smoke, radiant above the havoc beneath, winging in superb glory like a phoenix from its pyre, this wonderful creature of the mountains. My mind took refuge and comfort in the sight of her.

The phoenix, too, was a bird of the sun, larger than life. At the end of its cycle on earth, it sacrificed itself on a pyre so that a new phoenix might rise from the ashes.

I shook myself back to reality. Leaden weights seemed to anchor my feet to the ground. I dragged them up the gully, my throat searing. Tears of cold and misery froze as they left my eyes. My hands were raw. Snow packed thick and hard, too much for the fire.

The eagle swung into place over me and feeling returned. Although it was dangerous with her there, the sight of her was so familiar, so known, that the warmth of it broke through to me. She called in strong warning, as always, and was joined by her mate. "Is he still there?" I yelled, "is Temujin still safe?"

I struggled up, lungs laboring. How could she know of my longing for shrill assurance that the baby prince still lived? There was no way for her to tell me just what she had suffered. Whatever hardship came to her she would have to bear without sound, without comfort. No one would know of her grief, her desperation, her fear. She would hold her proud head high, hiding her hurt. Only her love and happiness were blazoned across the sky.

Her talons brushed my rucksack again and again because I was weary and slow, but at last I reached base. Smoke whipped in the wind. There was no sound from the aerie.

I made a dash for the edge and she was over me in a trice; then she raced over to Arthur in the gully and I had a chance to look down. Smoke seeped up through the aerie sticks. My heart stopped. But it was smoke I saw, coming up from the burning bushes below. Other than that I could see nothing. I dropped to my ledge and shielded my eyes from the sting.

Temujin's small body was stretched limp, awkward and unmoving. I shut my eyes, overcome. I whistled softly, more in requiem. The smoke curled and draped round the rock face as I caught a glimpse of the aerie, steaming in a cauldron of rock.

I looked again. The small form stirred. The talons on the outflung leg gently flexed. I whistled again, urgently. His eyes flicked open in recognition, then closed again. With a sleepy "cheep" he snuggled down.

He slept! In the burned shell of the earth round him, through the tearing anxiety for him of those that loved him, he slept. My defenses gone, I let the smoke do as it would with my shining eyes.

When Arthur arrived after a rugged journey of all-eagle attention, I called out to him, "This is Thanksgiving Day. Let's give them their dinner now." Arthur's face crinkled into a smile of relief. "I wish," he said, "that we could give them the equivalent of a bottle of champagne."

Warning sounds came from above. The wind blasted our eyes with cinders. None of it mattered anymore. Temujin lived! Our eagle family was safe. There could be room only for our thanksgiving.

> Nor shall this peace sleep with her; but as when
> The bird of wonder dies, the maiden phoenix,
> Her ashes new-create another heir,
> As great in admiration as herself . . .
>
> SHAKESPEARE

I belayed Arthur with a light heart. The eagle hung over me as he reached for the hide in the appalling wind. I waited. I could not understand why the eagle was slow to attack me when the direction of the wind favored a clean dive. Maybe I *am* a little crazy. But I like to think that she, too, felt we had both had enough heartache for one day, that she was also giving thanks in some eagle way. But would anyone believe me? People wiser than I might find a reason why she spread just above me, talons probing but without menace. They would have a difficult task convincing me that she could not have ripped down on me if she had wanted.

At last Arthur was down, and I held the rabbit up to her. She called imploringly, a call quite different from her normal confident voice. It was plaintive and said, to me, that her eaglet was hungry, that she wanted the food I offered, and soon; but please not to demand too much of her. So I put the rabbit on the nearby patch of snow that looked like a laundered tablecloth on a vast table of black.

The great body swung as we watched each other. Then, a moment later, without hesitation, and as a sweeping finale of music seemed to crash round us, she snatched up the rabbit, and was gone.

Temujin turned immediately when I whistled, wide awake now that he knew food was on the way. "My jolly, fat phoenix," I told him, "somehow between us we have the whole thing mixed up. You are supposed to be very beautiful, the epitome of a god, and look at your fat! You are supposed to be flying up there to the stars with the remains of your father, remember, and look at those stubby,

112

useless wings! But I cannot tell you just how glad I am that there are no ashes for anyone to rise from, and that you are still here."

Arthur looked at me, amused as always, at my talking to the eagles, my mimicry of their tone of voice and the personal translations I ascribed to their calls. "You are off your head," he said.

"Just to make you feel good and prove you're right," I answered, "I am going along to tell Temujin of my thanksgiving." Arthur dismissed me. "If the wind does not get you, the eagles will."

I hugged the growing body and could feel his first automatic tension lessen as he lay against me, his head beneath my chin, looking out on his world. Today, as on the day of his birth, a barely visible movement had towered into thanksgiving that he lived, this new-created heir from the mother I admired so greatly.

"Time's up," Arthur said anxiously. Then his voice rose: "Look out, here comes Mum with the dinner!" Her talons were occupied with carrying the food, and the aura of truce was still strangely about us as she reached the aerie and I the hide.

Temujin's wings were already fringed with fast-developing feathers. His legs were still trousered with wool, the parts of him with the least number of feathers sticking through. This seemed strange to me. Only a true eagle has legs feathered down to its talons, yet they were the last parts to develop. His talons were elongating, the tips sharp. He lay on his side and stretched each wing and leg to its fullest extent. He looked like a snowbird with spring waiting to burst through.

All for love, and nothing for reward . . .
SPENSER

He tore voraciously at the rabbit and his mother watched him for a moment. Then, for no apparent reason, she took it away from him and flew off, returning without it. She made a continuous clucking noise at him, and he lowered his head. He sulked, turning his back on her, not caring a rap for any food she did not want to give him. She scolded him but he was rigidly indifferent, so she called to his father and that worthy parent, important at the appeal made to him, fussed on the aerie and gave a clucking call similar to his mate's.

I smiled involuntarily. He could so easily have been saying, "It's not really worth all the fuss, let him have it." For she dropped from the aerie, getting in the last vehement word, but returned with the rabbit. Now she tried to get back her child's favor. But Temujin would have none of it. Unreasonably, she turned on his father and shouted at him. We had the embarrassed feeling that we were looking over someone's fence.

No sooner had his parents left him, still calling impatiently to each other, than Temujin began tearing at the meat, toppling over in his eagerness. A large piece threatened to choke him and involuntarily I moved to help him. "You have it bad," teased Arthur. The eaglet struggled with the bone in his throat, shaking his head, stretching out his neck. His rasping cries reached his mother and she alighted next to him. She made no effort to help, watching him unconcernedly as he tried to disgorge the bone. Eventually he succeeded and sat back exhausted. His mother promptly swallowed the bone herself.

I wondered about all the bone, fur and feathers he consumed with the meat; then I remembered that they formed into pellets, as they did with his parents; and which every so often they disgorged, retching to rid themselves of the indigestible material swallowed in their eating.

Temujin dozed after his meal, lying against the rabbit carcass. As we knew food would be even more scarce after the fire, we had also brought along a guinea fowl.

What had started out as a photographic mission expanded subtly over the weeks and months. It was important now, too, that Temujin should have food each week, to prepare him for the months ahead when he would leave the aerie. The layers of fat we were ensuring would be a reserve to keep him going during the lean times of his training. We found ourselves slogging up the mountain in treacherous weather, days impossible for photography or being near to the eagles, so that an eaglet would have one good meal a week.

He certainly was a glorious young eagle, and my pride in him was as great as that of his parents. "He's growing very handsome," I said. And Arthur, no doubt remembering the difficulty in raising food for him, said drily, "I am not surprised."

114

I Get a Twin, and Have a Game of Hide-and-Seek

Be sure of it; give me the ocular proof . . .
SHAKESPEARE

But for the wind the night had only the sound of whispering grass. As I lay in my sleeping bag the Milky Way was a carpet of daisies. At dawn I could see the twin spots of eagles above me. Large raindrops fell unexpectedly, puffing up dust where a week ago a sheet of snow had dazzled the black aftermath of the fire.

This early morning the eagles' love for each other was like music scored across the red bars of the rising run. It filled the dawn with meaning and I thought, wryly, this is how they catch me. They enmesh me in the beauty of their flight, then change from artists to predators much more adroitly than I can change from being bewitched to summoning any semblance of quick thought.

Arthur came up the valley carrying under his arm something that looked remarkably like me. The morning was alive with magic! The form had dark blue jeans and a blue sweater; it was my height. Although I do not weigh much, I was sure Arthur would not be able to cart me up a mountain like that in such undignified fashion.

He had been doing some thinking since the episode of my Zulu cap. What would the eagle do to me on the precipice edge if I did not always move just in time, he asked himself. To find out, he had made a hessian model of me. It would tell him exactly what would happen if I did not dodge out of the eagle's way.

I hated the idea. She was an eagle, true to herself. I was sure that when she whipped the cap off my head she had expected me to duck; when she dived she expected me to dodge. I had been careless, or unthinking, and she had just capitalized in true eagle way.

"You are making excuses for her," Arthur said. "She finds you a good risk, one that will not retaliate. Experience tells her that she has nothing to fear from you, but I am sure that knowing you, knowing all this, she will never pass up the opportunity to knock you over the edge. She won't be able to resist it."

"Exactly," I stalled, "you have answered your own question, so why don't we leave it at that?" But he was not to be put off.

Still imbued with the magic of the early morning, and taking refuge there, I glowered at my dummy jogging up the gully, slung over Arthur's shoulder. I let them go and went on my own in the direction of the peak and buzzard country. I was not quite ready for the dummy.

Later I reached base by way of the sunsplattered crags above it. She came looking for me, knowing I had not come the usual way. Seeing her, I hid in a tiny cave and watched her patrol back and forth. After a while I put my head out and she hissed from above, and shot up from the rock where she had been standing waiting for me to reappear. I dashed for another overhang, and she dropped down, following me. In this way we arrived just above base.

Arthur said later that it was like watching a comedy as she sat on the edge of the rocks above me, peering over to see if I was there. If she caught sight of me she bounced up, screaming. Sometimes she stood above an overhang and leaped up hissing to give every indication of having found me, and I shouted from another hiding place, "Go on, you old shyster, you're cheating!"

"I know you two dames understand one another," Arthur said, "talk to each other, scream together, sort things out. But I never thought to see two grown old birds playing hide-and-seek on a mountain top!"

During the morning's game I had forgotten the dummy, but there it was mocking me.

"How about putting it on the ledge where she had a go at you while you were recording," Arthur said. I still demurred. "It's like the blanket act all over again," I protested. "I really do hate playing a trick on her. I hate even more that she'll believe I am nothing after all but a woman of straw." Arthur chuckled but insisted.

I made my way to the ledge. The fun of the morning was swiftly erased as she frisked my back. It took me some time to set the model up straight. "Sorry," I called to her, "but this is by special request."

At last it was done. One of me sat inanely looking across the Drakensberg, accepting any fate the gods saw fit to impose. The other me, just as incoherently, could only stand and stare.

Before I had time to move, the eagle wheeled in. Wrapping talons round the sitting me's shoulder and back, she made off in an effortless upward arc with the unresisting hessian me. She looked down as though dumbfounded at what she was carrying, as well she might be. I swung there against the clouds, as heavy as she was, a forlorn puppet being bundled ignominiously along by airfreight. The aircraft didn't flap a wing! Contemptuously, she dumped the model on the butcher's block with the remains of her other victims.

Arthur was triumphant. His film was filled with the whole incredible scene. I felt incomplete, split in two, as though I was not sure who I was, and glad that the camera did not record my thoughts as my twin swung into space, glad I was not decapitated and brought in for Temujin's lunch.

At seven weeks he had stood in quiet dignity, showing off his feathers. I had not been sure, when I named him, what sex he was, not being expert at judging from the eggs. But as he grew I was convinced he was not another Cleo. He was very much like his father, unaggressive and serene. He and Alexander were similar, but Temujin was tempered more finely than his brother, and looked more regal. He had none of Cleo's brashness, and he got on with his mother much better than Cleo had.

Scraps of wool still hung all over him, but his wings were almost completely feathered, as was his back. His chest bristled with thrusting quills and there were small black feathers surrounding his eyes and ears. His wings were enormous; he used them to prop himself up when he ate. His development, especially in talons and feathers, was so rapid, so incredible, that I was sure if we stayed watching we would see the feathers growing, especially the primaries!

We were distressed to see the remains of a lamb on the aerie. I went to André and offered to pay for it. "I like your honesty," he laughed, "but don't worry. I saw the eagle get that lamb fair and square from the snowdrift, where it had died." The eagles, not normally carrion eaters, must indeed be finding food hard to come by!

Spring Comes to the Mountain

And in green underwood and cover
Blossom by blossom the Spring begins . . .
SWINBURNE

After the fire the burned nakedness of the earth was clad in faint green, and the mountain seemed on the brink of erupting into lusty life. Crocuses pushed their lovely way bravely through the cinders. Bushes, gaunt and leafless, changed into feathery wands, and flame lilies waved gay red trumpets. A new generation of lambs trotted dutifully at their mothers' heels. Bees hummed in the wild peach blossoms. Soon the charred earth would have a covering of petals. Icicles melted drop by glistening drop.

Temujin, too, was brushed by the first tide of spring. His new outfit was complete, all stray bits of baby fluff gone; even his legs were fully feathered. His head was the only part of him still a little woolly, making it look like a small boy's untidy hair. He was a young masterpiece, a true aristocrat. At two months he was larger than his parents, but he had yet to lose the layers of fat that would disperse during his training days.

His wings were glorious. He stretched them out in the sun and I examined them closely. The ten large primaries forming the wing-tip he could move individually, spreading and closing them like fingers. They were losing their baby solidness to become light and rigid. Now, as was his body, they were speckled in fawns, russets and browns. The indication of the black to come was there at the base of the feathers; but he would not be totally black, except for his white back feathers, until he had had four molts—in four years' time.

The primaries would remain off-white, the "windows" on his wingtips. These large, long, strong primaries would most often be tilted up to deflect the wind over them. On the upper side of his wings were the secondary feathers. They formed a complete bank, or "hand," which he would move as an entity, like the flaps on an aircraft. They would be used for lift and as a brake.

The tiny short alula feathers growing along the top of his wings would be his "pilot" feathers, giving him flight information about the thermals rising from the warm earth, the gales and breezes. Sensitive, attuned to every mood of the wind, they were Temujin's radar system, telling him when to glide, bank, spiral, race or soar. They would tell him when to change his flight, would gauge the direction and pressure of the wind, and warn him of its sudden vacuums. He would obey them unconsciously.

His tail had about a dozen feathers folded over like a fan; he would use it for steering. In contrast to the almost motionless stretch of his wings in flight, it would move constantly as Temujin angled it to the wind. From a lazy soar to a deep, downward plunge, his tail would not only adjust instantly, but would also act as a powerful brake, fanning out like a parachute to execute the spectacular drag that allowed him to stoop in on his prey without hitting the ground and then be propelled upward once again.

His parents gave a display of their unbelievable feats in the air. How easy it looked as we watched, earthbound, against the rock face—an eaglet whose wings would soon be as proficient as those above him, and I, who could but admire the effortless power making the wind work for them.

Now that Temujin was older and not as defenseless as he had been as a baby, his parents did not stay so much in the vicinity. They hunted farther afield and were often away for many hours at a stretch. Now, too, they ate part of the food we brought, whereas

Humans in an eagle world...

We encroached on their lonely world and gradually their natural resentment changed to an acceptance of our being there.

Peter recorded to perfection eagle screams and the eaglet's baby voice, and Arthur was photographer of the film For the Love of an Eagle, *which has won over six international awards.*

Always the old mother eagle stood guarding her own as we toiled up the mountain, and I was filled with the beauty and the strength of my splendid eagle friend.

Snow-covered vastness of the eagles' domain with Lesotho's ranges stretching to the horizon.

Arthur, on the escarpment edge, raises his camera in warning to a hunting eagle.

We get to know each other...

The mother eagle and I learned many things about each other and a distinct current of understanding grew between us. She surrendered none of the wild and arrogant huntress, yet some of her disarming actions were eloquent and rewarding messages of her trust. My admiration of her could only grow.

Sometimes I stood on the escarpment edge and she flew around me relaxed and unconcerned, greeting me in peace and great goodwill.

Arthur watched the two of us one day and said, "I am sure she does not like that cap you are wearing." Despite the cold, I replaced it with my normal hat she knew well, and she immediately whipped in and taloned the offending cap away.

The rabbits we brought belonged to her. If I tied the carcass to the top of my overloaded rucksack, she felt entitled to zoom down and help herself to it.

My twin is swung by an eagle into the sky...

The mother eagle always looked for the opportunity to remind us that we encroached on eagle territory, and sometimes, caught with little protection, I felt the quick thrust of talons.

Arthur constructed a life-size dummy of me and, despite my reluctance, persuaded me to carry it to the escarpment edge to find out what the mother eagle would do if I did not dodge and duck away from her. He had his answer when she flashed down and wrapped her talons round my inanimate twin's shoulder and back.

The dummy, as heavy as the eagle and five-feet high compared to the eight-foot spread of her wings, swung with her into the sky. She lofted it away with effortless ease, and dropped it on the "butcher's block."

Accolade from an eagle

In my third year of knowing her the mother eagle gave me, no matter how briefly, a precious thing. By showing her trust in accepting food from me, she gave me the accolade of her friendship.

She hung above me unmoving, watching me, making up her mind whether to take the food I offered.

Suddenly she hunched her great wing dropped legs and talons and dived towar me.

She plunged down, talons positioned for the strike. The food, I wondered, or me?

Almost upon me, her raucous voice was scream and I could see the sun dancing on he eyes.

The impact was tremendous as her talons, strongly and without hesitation, fastened to the rabbit. There was no fear in her eyes as she looked at me fleetingly before bearing off her prize.

Then she was away, her voice strident wit. anger at having bargained, after all, with th human for food. My heart soared as I watche her go.

'o Mr. and Mrs. Aquila 'erreaux, a son...

*a the second week of July, after
*e mother eagle had brooded them
*r forty-two days, one of the two
*gs hatched. In the world of black
*gles only one eaglet, or egg, was
stined to survive.

The aerie hung against a rock face on a spur in the Drakensberg Mountains. The sun reached it about mid-morning.

We knew, from previous years, that the mother's arrival with a green twig heralded the birth of an eaglet. The small-leafed branch seemed to serve the purpose of keeping sun from the baby and protecting it from flies.

Frozen, bedraggled, the eaglet struggled into the sun to thaw out and greet his world. A day old, it seemed to me impossible that this puny baby would one day become a replica of his strong, proud mother. I named him "Temujin," the boyhood name of Genghis Khan, known as "Rider of Heaven."

Left: *A week old, his eyes now wide open, he was surrounded by food, but not knowing what to do with it he shouted lustily for help.* Right: *His mother thrust bits of meat and bone into his willing beak. At two weeks he was always hungry.*

Below: *His mother fed him always with moving gentleness, completely absorbed in her task as she chose the best for him—liver, heart and muscle, with the right proportions of bone and fur.*

Above: *At three weeks, satiated, he lay drowsing beside the remains of the carcass that would be his next meal.*

Above: *When he was a month old he became adventurous, raising his stubby wings in a rush of joie de vivre.*

Left: *To avoid collapsing he propped himself up, but discovered that this was no way to reach the meat beneath his mother's talons.* Center: *He fell down to his knees and tugged impatiently at the carcass without success.* Right: *His mother, who had tolerantly watched all his efforts, shredded the food and nudged it gently against his beak. He did not gape in the way of other fledglings but always waited until the food was offered him.*

He lay in the sun, stretched his wings and flexed his strengthening talons. At six weeks, the quills of a week ago were recognizable feathers.

Tips of feathers showed through his woolly wings when he was five weeks old. His beak began to hook over and his eyes were aware under their hoods.

An eagle grows, and so does a friendship...

Temujin's growth was little short of spectacular. In his second month he changed from a fluffy toy with soft beak and talons into the shape and hooded look of an eagle.

After he had eaten, Temujin sat back, too full to move.

As Temujin grew so did our acceptance by the eagles. Temujin and his mother acknowledged our presence above them.

A ring and a spy…

When he was five weeks old Temujin had an identification ring put on his leg. This was inscribed "Notify Pretoria Zoo, South Africa. 658.007," and would assist if anything happened to this eaglet in the future study of black eagles.

Temujin watched unconcernedly as I made my way across the rock face to him.

The shadow of the father eagle hung above me. There was little danger from him, but we were sure, later, that he had somehow communicated with his mate. Mother was on the "butcher's block" with the rabbit we had given her and, from experience, we knew that I would have only a few minutes to go across the rock face before she returned to the aerie with food for Temujin.

The ring firmly in place so that i would cause no distress or threat, picked up my eaglet and hugge him. Below: The mother returne sooner than usual and rocketed to ward the aerie.

Alert, curious and a little wobbly, it does not seem possible Temujin will soon be flying! The more adultlike appearance in head and talons showed noticeably in his seventh week.

The eagle heir is halfway to flying...

At ten weeks Temujin stood, a prince of eagles, not yet ready to fly, but his body compact and strong.

Lost and found

Precipitated into premature flight by a fight between his mother and a jackal buzzard, Temujin was blown by the gale to the opposite side of the mountain.

The eaglet watched, terrified, at the conflict above him, then floundered away from it.

After a long search I found him, a tiny eaglet in an unknown, storm-ridden world, and he lay there exhausted.

I sat with him, whistling softly and talking to him, sounds he had known all his short life, and we were glad to have found each other.

I held him securely as he lay against me making no attempt to struggle, and we started on the long, steep way back to his home.

With a tired eaglet tucked under one arm, I slid down on the rope to the old aerie site where he would be safe until, in the morning, he could drop to his nest.

The chance of finding him on a vast mountainside seemed remote. I could only ask for a miracle.

When we had both rested, I went to pick him up but the buzzards dived down, frightening him into reeling farther down the mountain.

Once again I found him, far below, and this time I gathered him safely into my arms, overcome with relief.

I was overcome at having to leave him, but the darkening sky eventually forced me to swing up the rock face. Temujin moved out and stood there, a perfect eaglet, watching me go, and my heart seemed to break.

Clash of wills

Temujin's rigorous training to cope with the innumerable hazards facing an eagle would begin in earnest once he was flying, but he was taught a great deal of discipline while still bound to the aerie.

The eaglet developed a distinct personality and sometimes defied his mother. As he turned away from her, sulking, she shouted her displeasure.

Even when he was almost adult i stature, there were differences c opinion, and his mother called fc his father. Temujin watched him fl ing in with a mixture of defiance an trepidation.

Mother and son were reconciled, and tenderly nuzzled each other.

Father responded briefly to the call for help and seemed to say, "It's your fault. I have been allowed little to do with the boy."

All eagle, at twelve weeks, Temujin no longer needs any help from his mother to butcher the meat. Since his rescue the previous week he is more aware, watching every shadow and movement around him. This was the only time we ever saw a lamb on either aerie or "butcher's block." André, Eagle Mountain's owner, told us that he had seen one of the eagles swoop in on it where it lay in the snow, dead from the cold.

An eaglet spreads his wings

The third week after he had been rescued and returned to the aerie, Temujin stretched his wings in first flight.

During his last days on the aerie he seemed to brood as though conscious of leaving his birthplace, yet yearning for the world spread before him.

With startling suddenness he answered the call of the world that was his, and the call o his parents above him. At first inexpert, he kept to the protection of the rock face, but intoxicated with the rapture of movement, he soon made flying look wondrously easy.

Later he climbed to the he in an ardent sweep of w his eagle outline limne baby majesty against clouds.

The aerie has spring clean

Throughout the eaglet's time on the nest, the mother eagle had moods of domesticity when she dumped about heaving redundant branches overboard and refreshing the aerie with twigs and sprays of a mountain bush. She brooked no interference, nor would she accept any help from her mate.

For the past hour she had made Temujin's life a misery as she moved him out of the way of her spring cleaning activities. He was often underfoot, showing his resentment, and she turned on him when he protested. Below left: Father tried to play his part in redecorating the home, and flew in tentatively with odd pieces of stick and greenery; but, after he had beaten a hasty retreat in the face of her contempt, she tossed his contributions over the edge. Below right: Temujin was brushed with the tide of spring and his outfit was almost complete in browns, gold and black. He spent a great deal of time on his toilette. Only his beak showed that he was part of a killer family: it was stained with blood.

Last days with my eagle friends

I could only be richer for having known them, my world could only be better for having touched theirs.

They soared around me, beautiful, poignant, three eagles who had given me so much—an eaglet called Temujin, followed proudly by his father and mother.

I wanted to tell her a host of things; to explain how I felt about her; to thank her and say I would never forget her ... but the words choked in me at the sight of her standing there waiting for me.

The old mother eagle came over me in a breathtaking sweep of her wings to bid me farewell.

previously, even when Temujin was satisfied, the remains of it were left on the aerie next to him.

Never was heard such a terrible curse!
But what gave rise
To no little surprise,
Nobody seemed one penny the worse!

BARHAM

One day Arthur put the rabbit in a brown paper packet in his rucksack, because it was not deep-frozen and likely to melt.

We were standing on the rim, making ready to go down to the hide. "Where's the rabbit?" I asked, used to seeing it hanging from his rucksack. He turned the packet upside down, and there, of all things, lay the joint of meat destined for the Bowland family's Sunday dinner. The rabbit, no doubt, was still wrapped up on the kitchen table!

I burst into hilarious laughter. But Arthur was furious. "We may as well go straight home," he fumed. "Without food here, they will be away all day."

Poor Arthur! He laughed about it later on, but right then, with his main lure gone, how long would it be before the eagles came to the aerie? I felt sorry for the photographer in him but could not help chuckling at the thought of his wife having to improvise with a rabbit pie instead of a joint of beef.

"I am sure Dawn won't mine," I bubbled, "if I give the meat to the eagle."

Arthur snorted. "She'll take it," I assured him. "Remember, she has accepted skinned rabbit from me before." Arthur did not answer.

I placed the beef on the edge of the escarpment. "If you want any pictures of this," I warned, "there's not much time. The old lady has just returned and she is not likely to pass up this opportunity of food."

The female eagle swept over for a look at today's offering. If she thought it a little off, she gave no sign. "Arthur," I began. Still he stalled, not believing. Nor did I blame him. But nothing this old eagle did surprised me any longer. I knew she realized that, though furless and skinless, it was food.

121

She raced for the summit and flung herself down the slope in a hissing slash. She tilted her wingtip to avoid contact with my leg and casually, with one talon, lifted the Bowlands' Sunday dinner into the sky.

Temujin was delighted when he watched the beef being flown in sooner than it usually was, because it had not needed skinning.

It is for homely features to keep home . . .
MILTON

Spring was affecting us all. All around us was the perpetual wonder of a countryside bursting with living, a feeling of urgency that time was passing too swiftly. Temujin reminded us that he would soon be going by exercising his legs, strutting, jumping, and flapping his wings. He spent long hours just brooding over his world, and I was frantic at the thought of the empty aerie.

Spring was here. And this, to the mother eagle, meant that there was work to be done.

She moved clumsily about the aerie tidying it up. Temujin complained bitterly, and so from the air did his father. But she paid them no attention. She shoved her son about as she rearranged branches. Redundant furniture she heaved overboard. Sometimes as she scratched around and removed old bones and bits of fur, her large talons became entangled in the eaglet's feet, and he turned in anger. She stood no nonsense from him. When her mate tried to help, she scorned his assistance. He was left carrying twigs around as she refused to let him land with them.

When the aerie met with her approval she flew off and returned with twigs of green leaves to freshen the nest.

These moods of domesticity otally absorbed her. Her son cried his annoyance. The father flew around disconsolately, both of them longing for peace and quiet. When it came, they responded to her magnetic charm. She stood next to Temujin and gently nuzzled his neck. He oozed contentment. She flew with her mate as if imparting to him that she had labored on their aerie for the sheer joy of sharing with him the rewards of seeing their home in order. And he, happy in their togetherness, could not but believe her.

122

About this time, the mother eagle gave me further evidence of the splendid giant she was.

Since I had learned to "read the wind" she had seldom caught me out when she rushed at me. Often her wingtip brushed my legs, sometimes her talons managed a quick lift of my sweater, but I usually managed to anticipate her flight well enough to evade her.

Then the whole picture changed. One day I watched her start to come in. Her wings hunched and folded back. Her legs dropped like the undercarriage of an airplane, and air whistled as it tore against her wings. I turned to run.

I glanced over my shoulder, seeing the sheen in the rich black of her body, her eyes dancing with the red of the sunset in the split second it took to reach me. The light was snuffed out as giant wings wrapped round me, and the thrust of a forceful tail lifted me off the ground. From her open beak a raucous shout shrilled to a scream as her body crashed against mine and the air burst from my lungs. Feathers brushed roughly across my face and neck. I was smothered in the smell of them. Then, suddenly, daylight flooded back!

I rolled over. "Did you see that?" I called. "Look out," Arthur shouted, "she's all set again." Peter grinned in boyish delight. "All I could see of you was part of a foot."

"But did you see?" I persisted. "That eagle has figured me out. No one is going to tell me she does not think clearly. She does! Just as I have been studying her, she has worked out my height, watched my actions. This time she knew she would strike, making sure I stood in the arc of her flight."

I had nothing but admiration for this wisdom, nothing but tolerance for the way in which she had given proof of it. No talons had clawed my back, no beak had slashed my head. She had knocked me forward about two yards, the feel of her all around me. For a timeless moment her gigantic blackness completely obliterated the sun. I thought briefly of what she *could* have done.

I could still feel the "whump" in the small of my back as I watched her lazy patterns in the sky, calling as she came over me. And I wondered if she was giving herself a pat on the back or whether she was consoling me with rough affection, "It's all in the game, my friend, and I did not hurt you."

Trust one who has proved it . . .
VIRGIL

Yet another time, rabbit tied to my rucksack, we climbed in the pale light of dawn. I copied the voice of the mocking chat and heard his clear call of joy as he proudly showed off his shy mate. Powerpuff tails of hares bounced into dark shadows and hopped cheekily out again.

Once on the escarpment, and halfway to base, I crouched under the swooping eagle, waiting for her to pass over me. But this time she didn't. Heady with last week's success she snatched at the rucksack, pushed me forward, and I felt the rabbit bounce over my head to the ground, still attached by its cord. I slapped the rabbit back into position and hurried towards the base.

Just before I reached it, she suddenly appeared, bristling at the provoking sight of the food on my back. Talons stretched out, wings rushing, she came at me and I quickly curled into a ball. The eagle's only thought was for the rabbit. She dropped, missed, and I ran for cover.

I jumped under the tree at base. "She nearly took the rabbit off my pack," I told Arthur. It hung down from my rucksack and looked distinctly battered. Arthur did not accept things always at face value. I saw his amused disbelief, though he was too much of a gentleman to voice it, and I picked up the gauntlet in typical feminine fashion. "All right, do you want to see?" I asked.

He followed me back to the slope where the eagle had rushed me, alive to anything his magic might film, and set up his camera just in case my story was true! Why didn't I keep quiet, I thought, as I crouched again, wondering what would come next. But my eagle and I, knowing each other, gave Arthur his proof!

I could not see what was happening, but I was reasonably confident that the rucksack would afford me protection, and my head was safely tucked away. I waited and heard her calling from the summit, the beginning of her flight in toward me. It was weird waiting for something that might never happen, though feeling that it *could* happen any moment.

The sound of her screams filled my ears. I felt a thump, a tug, another tug and a snap. When I looked up, she was sailing away with the cargo of food by special delivery for Temujin. I glanced at Arthur. "I got it," he said with a satisfied nod of his head.

> *When I am grown to man's estate*
> *I shall be very proud and great . . .*
> STEVENSON

While the mother was away with the rabbit, I got Arthur down to the hide, then ran around to the angled slab of rock to look down at Temujin, knowing that one day soon he would be gone. Now I smiled my relief.

At ten weeks he was all proud eagle. The lustre of his feathers sheened to innumerable lights as he turned around in the sun. He was a young golden king standing very straight and as always, over the last weeks, I was struck by the newness of him!

His feathers, clean and flawless, were slotted in place. His talons, innocent of hunting, shone as they gripped the aerie branches. His head was regal and groomed, his eyes were deep and dark under yellow hooded brows. Everything about him bespoke pristine perfection. Only his beak was stained with the blood of his food.

When his mother came toward the aerie, she did not alight. Instead, she cruised back and forth, the rabbit in her talons, her beak open in a constant carping that puzzled me. It left Temujin unmoved. He turned away from the sound of it and refused to look at her.

Was she trying to instill in him the ambition and energy to fly? She pounded in, nagged and chastised him; then shouted for her mate, who came in and daringly tried to pull the rabbit free of her talons as she stood on it. She shouted at him, too, incensed at his bravado, and Temujin squeezed between them and the rock, distressed by the family squabble.

Eventually his father flew off and Temujin made a grab at the food. This was too much for the mother. To be defied by both her men! It was the father's fault, so she followed, berating him in bitter voice that boded him no good while Temujin, without further ado, began his postponed meal.

Later, while exercising his wings and legs, he flapped madly. Sudden gusts of wind hit the aerie, and he became momentarily airborne. The more he flapped in panic, the higher he rose. His outstretched wings beating in the wind created the draught and pressure that were stronger and higher than the pressure above his wings; and this is the prerequisite for flying! How could he know that the thing to do was to close his wings and so decrease the pressure? And even had he known, it is doubtful whether he yet had the muscle strength to fold his mighty wings back quickly. Only the fortuitous dropping of the wind and his tiredness returned him in a heap to the aerie.

Each time his mother flew over he stood nonchalantly inactive, as though careful to see that his parents did not get fixed ideas about his time to fly. He looked at her respectfully. She could not tell him when his wings would say "go," when his heart would exult in "now," when the sky would call exhilaratingly, "Come, it's time!"

After the altercation with the food, they stood together, eager for reconciliation, he lowering his chest to her in the eagle way of begging, and she in answering grunts and caws, telling him all was forgiven. His whole being was one of gentle confidence, one that told her, please not to be anxious about him, she would be proud of him one day, and he would not let her down.

> Bird of the broad and sweeping wing,
> Thy home is high in heaven,
> Where wide the storms their banners fling
> And the tempest clouds are driven.
>
> PERCIVAL

The valley, too, was filled with the sweetness of spring. An old Zulu shepherd whistled to his sheep as he gathered them together from amongst the rocks. They bleated complaints, but it was from habit, for the grass was lush, and the pace of the old man was in keeping with the tranquillity of the day.

126

"There is someone up there," I said to Arthur, pointing to a figure in an orange hat, khaki shirt and black pants standing against the side of the mountain above the escarpment. We were surprised. We had never seen anyone else up here. Did he know of the eagle that was antihuman? I was fearful for his safety, and wondered why the eagles were not watching him. Arthur was anxious that the presence of a stranger, someone the eagles did not know, would upset them.

By the time we reached the plateau, we could understand why the shepherd was concerned about his flock. The wind could change the whole face of the mountain world with devastating speed. It came now, blustering about the rocks, churning the peaceful clouds. The white masses looked like battlements with banners flying wildly, as though torn between wind and far-off lighting. We knew the mountain. But we could never anticipate the wind. The grass of the plain was no longer a tufted garden of intricate color and design. It lay like a wall-to-wall carpet, flat before the grueling wind. But for all that, we had to struggle to walk over it.

I looked up at the figure, wondering how he fared in the gale, and suddenly knew why, as yet, there was no sign of the eagles. Then, from where we stood, the whole angle of the figure changed and took shape. A clump of watsonia flowers had made a jaunty orange cap; a boulder, gray-green with lichen, a khaki shirt. Then a large female eagle gave black trousered legs to the whole unlikely apparition! Our laughter at ourselves was loud and long as the figure of the eagle found voice above the gully and called to us. She sounded almost as if she shared our joke.

On days of wind like this it was impossible to believe that the eagles could ride the sky. Since we could get nowhere near the escarpment edge, we gazed in rapture at the eagles' flying repertoire. It left us drained, but with deep respect. As if the eagles were not enough to fill our eyes, the buzzards chose the gale to buck over from their side of the mountain, spoiling for a fight. Scarcely able to stand upright ourselves, we felt the universe swing about the great birds, rejoicing in their element.

There would be little chance for photography, so I made my way, struggling against the wind, to a large boulder and held the rabbit up to the suspended eagle. My arm was mown down instantly by the force of the wind, and the rabbit went rolling down the slope. The female got to it first and lofted it away, but her mate, in the only time I ever saw it happen, challenged her for it, and a tug-of-war followed in which honors were even. Wandering round in the sky were two eagles, each toting half a rabbit.

This meant that two pairs of talons were safely pincushioned for a spell, so I crawled to the edge, hanging on to any available rocks and grass, to catch a glimpse of Temujin. He watched his parents carting his food above him. Was I imagining it or did his natural frown seem extra deep with disapproval?

My ledge was a cold cell of damp rock. Pebbles hurtled against me in a barrage of cutting chips. Freezing blasts turned my blood to ice. Temujin stood back against the rock as the gale tore at the aerie. When I whistled, his head stretched up toward me. We looked at each other, unable to offer any consolation, except that we were in it together.

His parents' landing was an extraordinary feat of controlled excellence. Imagine it! Treacherous wind thundering at solid rock, over seven feet of outstretched wings, light as a silken sail, caught up in its violence. And there they were, manipulating each feather, each bank of feathers, each segment of the fanlike tail, using every eddy and gust as they navigated their course. Just prior to the actual touchdown they stayed motionless directly above the aerie, waiting for the precise moment when wings and wind would be in complete accord. Then wings folded in perfect timing to bring them in a swift glide to their destination.

They arrived almost simultaneously as though on the same sweep of the wind, disengaged the rabbit halves and held firmly to the aerie as they leaned into the gale. With the shelter of rock and parents, Temujin was soon tearing hungrily at the food.

"Well done! That really was great," I cried.

They were happiest in the air and were soon pivoting the gale, illuminating the already electric sky.

> . . . *Welcome ever smiles,*
> *and farewell goes out sighing* . . .
> SHAKESPEARE

They rocketed down again and I saw that it was not aimless flight that brought them lower. They had a target in view. I watched, enthralled, as they flew in formation with a third eagle. Why did they not chase it away?

Then, "It's Cleo!" I shouted.

Cleo or Alexander? Cleo, surely. Alexander would be blacker. Cleo was just over a year old. They played with her, fussing to make her welcome. They were still some ways away from the rock face, but we could see them clearly. I looked at Temujin and he was watching them too. I was overcome with sentimental nostalgia to see the eaglet I had known so well flying above me. Cleo, who had been such lusty fun, was making out, flying happily with her parents.

Nature was not so harsh after all, I thought complacently, wrapped in warm, possessive pride that I knew them all. There flew Temujin's sister, or would she one day be his mate? Cleo had three years to go to maturity. Young Temujin had not yet flown. He had a lot to learn before he could think of setting up house.

Abruptly the picture changed. While the threesome had been flying in the clouds beyond the rock face, the scene was one of family togetherness, parents delighted to see a visiting child. But, once over the aerie, Nature erupted into its harsh acknowledgment that the time they were living in was now, not last year. That was gone. Below them was this year's offspring and he was their whole life. Nothing, not even last year's eaglet, must come anywhere near him. Having wandered harmlessly back and been welcomed to the territory where she had been born, Cleo now shied in fear as her parents turned on her and chased her away. She came again, unable to change so suddenly from their gentleness to this aggression. But they were blind to her entreaties and hounded her unmercifully.

"Leave her alone," I called, as Cleo flew away disconsolately. "The bullies," I cried, trembling with anger. How could they do it to her? How could they send her off into the unknown, their little daughter who was only fifteen months old, and who so obviously wanted their love and the comfort of her home?

I was shattered by the ruthlessness of it. "It's not just Cleo," Arthur said, "it's every eagle that ever lived. They expect it."

But I was not to be comforted. I was consumed with the awful thought that this would, one day, be happening to my eaglet, Temujin. Did he instinctively know this, as he watched Cleo disappearing into the gloom of the afternoon storm? Did he view his future with apprehension or was he longing to take it full tilt, with its soaring joy as well as its hardships?

Lost in a Hostile World

Something lost behind the ranges.
Lost and waiting for you. Go!
                    KIPLING

Often, over the weeks, buzzards invaded our eagle territory, seemingly always looking for trouble. Standing together on the rocks, the eagles were not willing adversaries, and maybe it was this that infuriated the buzzards. The eagles ducked and angled their heads away from the extended talons, and did not bother to leap into the fray the buzzards invited.

Although their flight is similar to that of eagles, two things to me were noticeably different. I never saw an eagle hover. They hung on the wind. But the buzzards had a distinct hovering movement. Also, they did not use their primary feathers as the eagles did. The long wingtips did not tilt up, nor did I ever see the feathers spread out separately to use the wind. Where the eagles were full of aerial grace, the buzzards looked brisk and busy. Often I would say, "Here comes the buzzard express," as they honked across the skyline, like noisy steam engines.

It appeared to be the male eagle's job to keep the buzzards in check. He patrolled the dividing line—the mountain summit—of their respective territories. Since he had spied on me while I was ringing Temujin, I held him in higher esteem. He was all for peace,

131

but I had no doubt that he would attack if the situation demanded it.

Looking at him now, he was no defender of the realm. He leaned against his mate in beatific bliss as she probed his feathers; and he hissed in obvious displeasure at the untimely interruption when the buzzards dived down at them. At this moment his love far outweighed his duty.

Did the wind blow throughout the week, I asked myself, or did it start up especially for us each day we came? There was no slackening in its force, no respite from the grit and grass it constantly hurled at us.

I wondered if Temujin caused his parents concern. I had the feeling he might. He was not yet twelve weeks old—too young yet to fly—but he looked so complete that perhaps they felt he could safely take his first plunge into flight. His feathers still appeared heavy with "baby fat" in the quills, and they lacked the light rigidity that makes an adolescent eaglet into a master of flight. The previous week his parents seemed to bully him a little. Now they showed indifference. Temujin gave no sign of minding, knowing his time was not yet.

When Arthur was down in the hide, I took the rabbit and climbed to the summit for a view of the circle of ranges and the glory of the sky.

I held up the food, offering it to my eagle friend. As always, she circled, spinning her flight round me and filling my ears with the sound of her cry as she came in closer to my upstretched arm. The gossamer strand of friendship hung between us. This eagle and I had absorbed much about each other without knowing it . . . two females who had been sorting each other out, ready to give and take, each from the other's world.

But now as she came the thread snapped as the gale flung at us both, and the buzzards bristled in with it to shatter the moment.

Yet somehow I knew it would not be my last chance. Her whole attitude had been one of simple, total trust, and only the final move toward me was needed. This thing that I had quietly believed possible three years ago had grown between us almost unnoticed in the remorseless necessity for her to be herself.

When she screamed up to meet the buzzards I was only dimly aware of their bitter feud. Overwhelmed by the voluntary nearness of her, I started to walk down the slope, my walk suddenly turning into a wild scramble as the duelists flashed swordlike talons all around me. The rabbit went flying. As I jumped headlong between the fringe of boulders, the eagle swooped in without hesitation to claim the prize.

Gone was the aura of serenity of a moment ago. Now it seemed a dream. Rushing down, I found Arthur waiting patiently on the hide ledge. "The buzzards seem to have the real screamers today," he shouted. "It is all I can do to keep the hide in place in this wind. Why don't you come down. . . . *Look out!* . . . *Look out!* . . ." His voice was like a whip. I covered my head quickly, expecting the accustomed whistle of wind and the blur of a jet black projectile past my ears. There above me the air broke into a wild turmoil of flying feathers and discordant sound.

Looking up, I saw the eagle and buzzard in savage fight, rocketing down to the plain. The rabbit over which they fought was forgotten. It fell unobtrusively among the rocks. As they were about to hit the earth, two sets of mighty wings spread and broke their falls. Then, disengaged, they launched their quivering bodies in upright strength to the clouds again, where, like feathered demons, the buzzard raged, bent on razing the eagle's back, while she turned upside down extending her powerful legs. The mates of both birds added their weight to the battle. Talon to clawing talon, beak to beak, they lunged at each other in hissing fury.

I looked down to the aerie.

"He's gone," I cried to Arthur, who was crouched on the ledge below. He swung his eyes to the nest. It was empty!

Then I saw him. Temujin! A floundering eaglet. His body staggered and bumped, his wings flapped a frenzy of desperation as he fought for some semblance of balance in the tempest. All the patiently practiced training on the aerie was meaningless. An unknown horror dragged him along, thrashing him against the rocks. He called out in terror. And it broke the heart-stopping paralysis clutching at me, as I caught a last glimpse of his flailing body sucked into the vacuum of a ravine that cut toward the summit.

My mind was a blank until a stinging blow cut across my neck. The crazed mother exploded in a shock of fear and anguish about me. Like the eaglet's forgotten lessons, gone was the normal code

133

of behavior between her and me, for it was obvious she thought we were the cause of the empty nest. She was blind with anxiety. She rushed me and I was unable to protect myself in the face of such determined talons.

I could not tell her she was wrong, could not explain that it was the fight that had frightened her son off the nest, the sudden falling of locked bodies straight past him that had precipitated Temujin into floundering off in sheer terror before he was ready to fly.

This time it was her or me!

The return of the buzzards saved me. The eagle's deadly strike at me curled upward to meet them. And I ran. I ran with the picture of a speckled body across my eyes. Arthur was still on the ledge. As I raced round the curve of the escarpment he yelled, "Where are you going?" The wind tore at the sound as I answered, "I'm going after him."

I hoped Arthur was safe; he certainly did not look it on that narrow ledge, hanging on to the rock and fighting the wind.

"No!" he countered, "no! It's clouding over, there's snow coming up and you will never find him. It's impossible. The mother will tear you to pieces."

I knew all that, knew he was right. But, like the mother, I was also blind—not with anger or anxiety, but against reason. I was blinded by a flame of knowing what I had to do. To ask me to leave Temujin was sheer madness. This was my eaglet. Temujin, whom I loved. He was part of me.

Somewhere he cowered, windswept, afraid, probably in buzzard territory, waiting. For what? The lonely darkness without the familiarity of his home and his parents, with slinking wildcats and jackals looking for a meal. And what was easier than a defenseless, terrified, half-grown eaglet? Oh no, I thought, it is not going to end here, not if I can help it. Temujin had given me hours of joy. I would not abandon him now.

"You go on down if you want to," I called out to Arthur. "He must be somewhere and I must find him. He is our responsibility."

I ran, not knowing where to begin. The ravine yawned cold and menacing and howled with the gale's demonic fury. Then suddenly I was unconsciously reading the wind. I followed its rampaging course to the summit and was boisterously shoved along as its gusts beset my back. This was the only way Temujin could have been blown. He would not have had a chance against this wind; he would have to go with it.

When I reached the far side of the mountain I realized the odds offered me—the enormity of trying to find an eaglet on a huge mountain. All around me was a sunless immensity of heaped masonry far more threatening than the side holding the aerie.

The black chill biting into me was from cold fear. For Temujin the eaglet, and for myself. In the sky countless Cape vultures smothered the small, low-lying clouds. To camouflage my racing pulses I looked at them defiantly. If you are waiting for Temujin and me, I thought, you are going to wait forever. Beyond them was the blue infinity showing briefly through the shifting clouds.

> *Whatever a man prays for,*
> *he prays for a miracle . . .*
> TURGENEV

I looked at that great vault, always there, as a man looks when most he needs a miracle.

Here, where I stood, the gale shook the mountain into stones and rocks that rattled and rumbled down its sides. Then it was momentarily silent, as though to look over the trophies won.

I could make little of the wind. It seemed to swirl in all directions. Shivering, I crawled about jutting promontories, my eyes searching the appalling scene. Bushes shook and grass danced crazily to the deafening music of falling stones in wild castanets. I ran down spurs, was hurled back, to go on again. And I ran again, sure the eaglet would be somewhere on the slopes between the summit and the edge of the rock face. There was no sign of him.

I tried again to sense the direction of the wind that had blown Temujin aloft as I crouched, now almost defeated. Overhead, the buzzards bustled and honked, dipped over me, to turn and come in again. The world heaved and wheeled until I felt I would be torn apart. It was full of mighty movement, elemental in its grandeur. In it I suddenly saw something quite different, something alien in smallness and gentleness there in the surging mass.

It was the quick flick of an eye.

Temujin! He looked up at me. How small he was against the

135

towering magnitude. His body heaved with punishment. His eyes flashed in dread. I went to him, whistling as I went, sat next to him and talked, and we rested together in the center of the whirlwind, my love for him an ache.

For the time being he was safe, and I knew where he was. I glanced briefly in thanks to the piling clouds from whence had come my miracle.

It was still light and the eaglet would not move of his own volition; he was too exhausted. The rocks protected him against direct buzzard attack.

Should I leave him and fetch Arthur, who would want to be here now that I had found Temujin? Or should I try to take him back with me? Would it be stretching my miracle? Would it, Temujin? He had known me his whole life and he looked at me now, answering my question. I knew he would be there when I returned.

"I've found him," I cried.

I told Arthur Temujin was lying on the other side of the mountain, and warned we would have to hurry against the threatening weather. I can only think that the flame of the miracle still burned and took me back over the mountain, for I have little recollection of it.

Then, as we started, the eagle pair dashed after us. Seeing me, the female skimmed my head. "She's missed you," Arthur panted, "she really does miss you."

But I was angry with her. "Why didn't you come after your baby?" I accused her. It was only when we reached the top that I realized why.

The buzzards had attacked in force and the eagles had made for home. There were territorial rules on both sides.

When I moved to pick Temujin up, his eyes flickered past me as the buzzards zipped over us. He turned, tormented, and floundered away again as he had done before.

This time the speckled body was hurled down into the depths of nowhere. The wind caught at his wings like sails. And he, knowing little as yet of their inordinate capabilities, could only let himself be carried along, unable to make his wings work for him.

Helpless, I watched his fearsome journey spin and roll him until I thought I saw him come to rest far below. I sat quite still in a silence more thunderous than the turbulence around me. I tried to conjure up "this sudden strength that catches up men's souls," but I had little strength left for myself, let alone enough to "rear them up like giants in the sky." I thought bleakly of an exhausted eaglet. I tried to return to the hour of wonder when his mother first betrayed her gentle love for him and I had promised myself that if I drenched my mind with the beauty of the eaglet, it would be a strength, a harvest, when most I needed it. I needed it now. But I felt beyond bringing in any harvest, even the rich one of my eaglet down there in the shadowed valley. I felt nothing except, perhaps, the dogged necessity to keep going.

After the buzzards had disappeared I picked up their circling above the distant slopes below. "You could not have done more," Arthur said quietly, full of sympathy, getting ready to face the journey back to the aerie side of the mountain, and home. I nodded, too beaten right then to argue. But he was wrong. I *could* do more! And I would go on! All I needed was a little time.

Tameless, and swift, and proud . . .
SHELLEY

I looked up, too tired to ask for a second miracle. The world seemed cold and lifeless compared to the sky's vivid face. The eagle flew high above the line of the escarpment. She courted danger, but still she came. When she reached me she banked, as she always did, and planed in lower. I was beaten, yes! I could not see very well —joy and tiredness have this effect on you—but the proud, imperial outline of wild strength came winging over me and gave me the greatest gift of all. Courage.

She alighted on a tall column, restlessly moving from foot to foot. Then, cawing in the way I knew so well, she lifted her great old head and shouted at me. Something like, "Well, why are you just standing there doing nothing? Why are you not looking for our eaglet?"

I was dazed with the wild wonder of her as I complained, "How can I look for anything, see anything, when you make me feel like this?" But I had already started to go. "You women," Arthur said, "what will you be up to next?"

Leaving the wind to carry away his protests, I hurried down the mountain, backward and forward along the escarpment edge, looking for a way to negotiate the rock face. It was sheer and dangerous. At last, in desperation, I reached out unsteadily to the branch of a giant yellowwood tree and climbed down it to the ledges beneath. The buzzards looked me over, then returned to their circling far below.

The shape and layout of land and rocks are never the same close up as they look from afar. I had been sure I would know where Temujin had been blown, that I would recognize the spot as soon as I arrived there, but I was hopelessly out in my reckoning. I had no idea where to begin and I still had a great deal of rock scrambling to do. Added to that, I suddenly had to contend with the buzzards as they flashed over me. They did not present much danger since the rocks around me were large enough to deflect a strike, but their presence prevented me from giving undivided attention to finding Temujin. And I knew it had to be soon.

For now the sun had gone behind the clouds. Its glow would still allow us some time, but not much. I could see Arthur, weighed down with camera and rucksack, sliding down a stony gully he had found to the side of the rock, hard going with that heavy burden.

But where was Temujin? Had the buzzards killed him and were they now transferring their harrying to me? Then, in a flash, an idea came to me. I found two enormous rocks tilted together. Crawling beneath them, out of sight of the buzzards, I watched while they fumed overhead looking for me. They honked their frustration. But when they could not find me, they flew purposefully toward the slope I had seen them circling earlier. Now they dipped and dived over a rocky shallow. The ruse had worked! They had pinpointed Temujin for me!

> *They that wait on the Lord shall*
> *renew their strength; they shall*
> *mount up with wings as eagles . . .*
>
> ISAIAH

I rushed down and gathered him into my arms, oblivious of the buzzards, burying my face in his feathers, making his neck damp with the relief that flooded me. Arthur tied his handkerchief lightly round Temujin's talons and, with my sweater over his head, I carried him on the long climb to his home. He settled comfortably against me, neither struggling nor showing any anxiety. Sometimes, unable to resist it, I looked down at him beneath the covering, at his fierce profile that belied the naked fear I had seen in his eyes, that still echoed in his thudding heart. And he returned my look steadily. His eyes were dark pools of trust in me.

The pathless mountain which before offered nothing but defeat was now illumined with the radiance of a new miracle, and I knew a rush of gratitude.

We made our way slowly to the summit, leaving the borders of buzzard territory to make for the domain of the eagles, a gale-torn, darkening world that was home. Though he would soon forget it all, and me, I would remember him forever. As I hugged him, his talons tightened on my wrist.

Now, with the goal in sight, I was overcome by the fear that I might be cheated at the last moment, so weary was I that my feet could scarcely cope with the simple task of putting one in front of the other. Arthur felt that I had done enough, that we should leave Temujin on the escarpment edge safely in eagle territory. "His parents will find him and look after him," he suggested, "now that he is in a world they all know."

The light was going fast, but I knew I had to get the eaglet down to the vicinity of the rock face he knew, even if it was only to the old nest site ledge we used as the hide. The escarpment offered little or no protection and I felt that, once against the rock, his mother could take over. After all that had happened to him, I was sure he would be too terrified to try to make his own way down to the aerie.

I stood next to the belaying rope expectantly. I had never roped up before to go down to the hide. But now, with a young eagle under one arm, it would leave me with only one hand to help me down, and I could scarcely stand against the wind as it was.

Arthur, around on the curve of the escarpment, looked momentarily puzzled as I waited, knowing I was averse to ropes. Then he proved that he was all photographer. He had carted a heavy camera all over the mountain, and my admiration for this feat grew to profound respect when he reminded me of the team spirit we had relied on for so long. He said, "If you are determinedly crazy enough to insist on going down there, I am afraid I am going to be crazy enough to film it."

Throughout the day, I had been unconscious of the camera in

my absorption with Temujin. Now I realized that what had happened today was a sequence of events that would not ever happen again. Arthur would be able to film the actions of the eagles in their natural everyday life, as he had been doing. But today could never be repeated. He knew this, and knew, too, that later on I would agree with him. I am grateful that he thought for both of us then. Glad, too, that he relied on my honesty about saying "no" if necessary, and my capacity to look after myself.

He told me later that when he saw me standing there with Temujin and looked at the drop below, he changed his mind. But by this time I had accepted that he was right. I nodded as I loosely knotted the rope round my waist. I could not rely on it, but the end tied to the piton would afford me something secure for my free hand as I slid down.

Exposed to the full force of the eagle he called "Mum," Arthur was in a precarious position with little protection. I glanced at her swoops over him and thought, "Atta girl. You concentrate on him. He can look after himself. Just give me enough time to get down."

> *Shoulder-high we bring you home,*
> *And set you at your threshold down . . .*
>   HOUSMAN

I try not to think too much about the swaying nightmare that took Temujin home, the eaglet under one arm and a series of burning jerks on the hand gripping the rope. I remember reading somewhere that love is a bulwark against fear. Love of a fierce old eagle and her silent, anxious mate? Love for the eaglet, Temujin, accepting with quiet confidence whatever I proposed to do with him? It must have been so, for fear was not the feeling surrounding me. I had this one thing to do. There was room for nothing else.

I heard Arthur's voice keeping Mum at bay. And then, intent to the exclusion of all else on what I was doing, I marveled as she divided her attention between us. I could not tell the full extent of the danger to Arthur. But I knew that the wingspan brushing my back now was only the continuation of her arc over him. No talons searched for a hold. To my weary mind, her cries seemed to be tinged with a note of encouragement. She could have knocked me off the rock face with ease, defenseless as I was, but the strike never came.

At last I was down to the hide ledge with my eaglet. I felt satisfied about his safety there. In the morning he could easily make a flying jump to the aerie. I uncovered his head and he started up in surprise. I put my hands round his folded wings, whistled softly and said, "You're home, adventurer." He looked at me, quieted, then sank down. I faced him into the corner of the ledge and held him awhile. Then, slinging my sweater round my neck, I caught at the rope and leaned out to go, trying to quell the desolation welling up in me as I made to hoist myself up.

Hanging there, midway between the escarpment and Temujin's ledge, I saw him lean out to watch me. He did not take his eyes from me, and I found I had no will or strength to leave him. My resolution melted at the sight of the look that said, "After all we've been through, you really mean to leave me?" But I *had* to go. Snow clouds were piling up angrily and we would have to walk down the mountain in the dark. How could I leave, with an eaglet watching me go and wondering how I could do it?

I felt a stab of defiance. He was right. I could not go just yet. Good-byes are not said in a moment. I dropped down again and sat with him, this frightened little eaglet who had come home, and who was now giving me much more comfort than I him. I would never be as close to him again.

I tried to whistle the old jaunty tunes of gladness that had always said so much, but the effort died in my throat. I shook my head wearily, not knowing what to think, what to do. "I have to leave you," I said many times. But the words refused to be translated into action.

His mother dropped to our level and winged to and fro past the rock face. She called, a halfhearted croak, as though she were as tired and despairing as I was. And her alien gentleness was almost more than I could bear.

"Look after him," I called, and blindly left Temujin to his parents.

I needed every ounce of remaining strength to heave myself up on the rope. At the last ledge I looked back at him. He had moved out again the better to watch me, and he stood there, a perfect

141

creature, his proud little head tilted up in puzzled loneliness at my going. His grave eyes held mine. Temujin, Temujin!

The gale swirled round me. Two eagles rode the storm-torn clouds high above. As I reached the top I put my head down on the hard rock. So long pent up, my heart just broke.

Accolade From an Eagle

I watched my foolish heart expand
In the lazy glow of benevolence,
O'er the various modes of man's belief . . .
BROWNING

Throughout the week my mind was filled with thoughts of him.

Remembering my unhappiness at leaving Temujin, Arthur tried to anticipate the disappointment he was certain was coming to me and tried to soften the blow. I was grateful for his concern, but refused to accept the root of it.

"You know, youngsters returned to a nest by humans are often rejected by their parents," he warned, "and it is possible that after you had left him he would try to move."

I could see what was in Arthur's mind: a Temujin lost again, trapped or injured somewhere on the mountain. It was not my vision. Reason had nothing to do with how I saw my eaglet, only unwavering belief. Arthur, sensibly, had fears for Temujin's chances. But I had none. "I was part of a miracle on that mountain," I told him, "and I am not turning my back on it now."

To return there I started out alone well before dawn, needing the peace the heights gave me. Because I had time on hand I climbed around the highest point, a long way from the aerie. Here

143

the wind was a roar, and I took refuge in a tiny cave with a pair of large hares that twitched suspicious noses but waited quietly with me until the sun gushed gold from the horizon, splashing its splendor around us with such a generous hand that I caught my breath at the lovely earth, frantic with wildly nodding flowers.

How could I want to keep Temujin earthbound for my sake, when his freedom could wing him over this glorious Basotho blanket of color rippling before me? Desolate at his going, how could I think of denying him the rapture of his shadow racing over this?

I felt a little smug that I was here on the mountain without the knowledge of the eagles; they could not have seen me start out in the dark. For all that, I missed the black forms I knew so well. The sky was incomplete without them.

Fighting my way to the top, I looked up automatically as I pulled myself through the large slabs guarding the summit. They were there! I wondered how long they had been watching me, how they had found me. Like golden arrows they shot down, and there was a shout of recognition as the female whipped past my head. What a heartwarming feeling to be greeted by a friend!

They trailed me right around the mountain, through buzzard territory, floating near me in companionable silence. Once they streaked across the summit in the direction of the aerie. I looked at my watch. It was not possible that they could have seen anyone approach the mountain from the opposite side, for we were below the summit, yet it was the time Arthur, and perhaps Peter, would be reaching the gully. I verified later that the eagle guardians had been above them when my two teammates reached the point of welcome, and had then made for buzzard territory. How had they known they were there? I could only marvel that they had.

As there was no sign of the buzzards, I concluded that the eagles knew of their temporary absence as well as the arrival of the humans. I dropped down through a rock funnel and made my way, past the rock face, along the length of the plain toward the gully. My belief was still intact that Temujin was somewhere near his home. Yet I procrastinated, letting my eyes wander everywhere but the place I most hoped he would be—the nest.

At last I looked there. No eaglet stood on the aerie.

A friend may be reckoned
The masterpiece of Nature . . .

Arthur and Peter looked at me sympathetically when I arrived at base. "He must be somewhere," I said quietly, knowing they must have seen the empty aerie, and Arthur said firmly, "You have to give up sometime, Jeannie."

But not yet. I did not want to think. "Shall we give her the food?" I suggested in a matter-of-fact tone. "She may give us a clue where Temujin is."

Arthur shook his head. "May as well," he agreed, with a finality that seemed to close the book.

He demurred as I started for the summit slope, never quite understanding my single-hearted wish for a tangible gesture of friendship from the mother eagle, a wish to draw in the vastness of the sky so that no barrier remained between her world and mine. She knew me, and this strong bond alone would make the initial decision possible.

Arthur gave his customary caution. "She'll be driving down at over one hundred miles an hour with a force that will knock you flying. That is, of course, if you can persuade her to come in to you . . . ," he added with a shrugging smile.

There seemed nothing in the world but the two of us as I swung up the food and she flew over to circle and call plaintively. The current between us was there, distinct and strong. I was asking her to make a decision utterly alien to her eagle makeup, to bridge the unfathomable gap between us with trust and friendship.

Then, never taking my eyes from her, I realized that the throb between us did not emanate entirely from my own yearning. Previously, every time I had held out the food, I had known somehow that I asked too much of her; that, though I had always hoped, her attitude told plainly that she had no intention of granting so impossible a request. But now she contributed generously to the tenuous current. It was she, I knew, who gave promise of its fulfillment. The decision would have to be hers alone. I stood and waited.

She floated down. Her talons moved as if exploring the wind. She hung, wings rigid, her whole body as taut as a strung bow.

Despite the thumping of my heart, a calm awareness was about me. Three years of great love for this glorious creature were about to soar into something inviolable, lit with wonder and meaning. Without warning she sped upward, spiraling in ecstasy as though filling herself with freedom before offering a bond of friendship. I did not move. Then she was back, gliding in, veering off, calling constantly. My heart warmed to her. She so obviously could not quite make up her mind to take the final plunge.

Still I waited.

She swept past me, did a quick wingover, returning behind me as if drawing an invisible ring around me. Satisfied that I did not move, she began to ring up, up, almost out of sight, and hung there, unmoving, filling the sky as she dropped, hard, straight and very fast. Wings folded, she came at me head first. Then, in a lightning change, her talons turned toward me, looming ever larger, searching, spreading. They zithered as they cut the wind. Now it was talons that filled my sight.

Was it to be the food? Or me?

She shouted as her unerring talons shot down, gripped the food and wrenched it from my hand. The strike was clean and sure. It came with explosive force, her wise old eyes fierce with concentration, but without fear. For a moment, her wings curled over my head and slashed my shoulder as she tilted and straightened out for the upward curve. My ears thrummed with the rush of wind. I spun around, reeling with the impact, and blood welled from a rip in my wrist.

Then, with a triumphant turn of her lovely head, she was away, her voice strident in message to me that she had after all this time decided to sacrifice a little eagle dignity to bargain with a human, to give me what I wanted.

My being soared with her and I was deeply stirred. I had waited for three years. Now I was rewarded. This old eagle had given me, at long last, no matter how briefly, a most precious thing as she winged in and touched my shoulder. She had given me the accolade of her friendship!

> *But the race remains immortal,*
> *The star of their house is constant . . .*
>   VIRGIL

146

Where would I begin to look for Temujin this time? The task seemed impossible, but I surged with the thought of yet another miracle, so recent, and the Flaming Terrapin's sudden strength was rearing me up with my giants in the sky. I could not leave the mountain until I knew where he was.

I started with the aerie. There was no alleviating its awful emptiness as I crouched on my ledge, memory a lament on the skirling wind.

Once again it was the flick of his eye, a sudden movement so small yet so vitally alive against the somber inanimate rock. He stood quite still, merged into his background, a statue of beautiful lines set into a niche on the ledge beyond the aerie.

Temujin! An eaglet lost and found, watching the human so much a part of his life.

Happiness roared in my ears. My heart sang.

An Eaglet Spreads
His Wings

The following weekend the mountain was lashed with rain, and as we saw its featureless bulk rising before us, we balked at the long, sodden walk ahead with sleet stinging our faces and hands.

It was two weeks since Temujin's rescue and I knew there was food for him in Arthur's rucksack. "It must be catching," he grinned, rain pouring down his face. "Somehow I do not doubt that your eaglet will be somewhere around."

At the gully a bedraggled mother flew clumsily over us as we slithered in the mud, eventually to pull ourselves over the rim. She labored past us as we made our way slowly along the escarpment. Water rushed down from the summit in innumerable rivulets to splash out in an icy waterfall over the edge. Every step was treacherous.

"When we find him," I said, "let's just leave the food and go.

They are having difficulty in keeping airborne, and hunting for food must be very difficult."

When we find him! The deluge had found its way through my anorak and down my neck. My feet squelched in my shoes. If he had already flown he could be anywhere. Yet find him I meant to do.

What ardently we wish,
we soon believe . . .

YOUNG

From base I went to he aerie rock face with my binoculars, ready to scan every segment of the mountain face I already knew so well. I dropped to my ledge, trying vainly to whistle while rain poured into my mouth. The mother flapped forlornly over me, both of us wet and cold.

The rain was whisked in all directions by the wind, but sometimes there were less violent eddies and I chose these moments to examine the rock-face ledges. I had to find him—and was so sure I would that every outcrop of rock seemed to be the figurehead of an eaglet.

His mother stood on the escarpment above me and I shouted, "Why don't you show me where he is?" She dipped over me, then curved back into the aerie.

He was there all the time! He stood against the rock, his head stretched into the rain tha coursed down his feathers. The aerie was dripping and cheerless, but I thought him a young king on a throne!

Fortunes . . . come tumbling into
some men's laps . . .

YOUNG

Three weeks after I had brought him home we plodded up the mountain on a day brilliant after a rain we knew had lasted throughout the week. Clouds piled on the horizon beyond the Drakensberg peaks, but the sky above us was vivid blue.

How could I expect him still to be at the aerie? Surely the miracle must have expanded to its limit! Even allowing for the understandable reluctance to move after his terrifying experience, he was nearly fifteen weeks old, and I felt sure his parents would now have a say in the matter of his flying.

Whenever I came from among the boulders of the valley and stood on the plain with my first view of the rock face and summit, I felt that I looked on something very belonging, very lovely. This was the home of my eagle friends, where I was now accepted, and I gulped with the delight of knowing them.

Both parents spun over us at the top of the gully, and I said to Arthur, "I think I'll give her the food straightaway. It's worth a try that she might take it straight to Temujin."

I moved up the slope to an outcrop, holding up the food to her. She was cautious and flew round me, drawing circles closer, to rise again at the last moment, then start all over again.

Had she had second thoughts about our friendship? Or did she wonder why I was offering the food here at the gully? Now I could feel the flow between us, and knew the bond was intact as we were caught up in the center of the maelstrom, oblivious of everything but the movements of one another.

She was a wonderful sight as she hung there in the void, this magnificent old lady who knew into the core of me. And now I saw that she was not afraid, but was assessing the best way to ge at the rabbit against the force of the wind.

Without warning she screamed down, and at that moment my arm tired and I lowered it. Seeing her dive in, I quickly raised it again, and she tipped the rabbit to knock it from my grasp so that it bounced down into the grass.

I was concerned that he suddenness of my actions might put her off, might make her sense some sort of a trap. But she rose above me and her whole being seemed to say, "Let's get on with it. Once I have made up my mind about a person I do not change it."

She was impatient. Her talons loomed larger. Her lovely wings, taut against the sky, were fringed with gold. Her wonderful old head, open-beaked with raucous savagery, still managed to convey through flashing eyes her eloquent awareness that she had nothing to fear. Nonchalantly she swung the food aloft, and I held my breath waiting to see where she would take it.

My disappointment when I saw the powerful huntress making for the butcher's block was short-lived. By the time we reached base she was back again making for the aerie, and so was I, running and shouting my joy.

> . . . *he could never recapture*
> *The first fine careless rapture. . . !*

She carried the food round in the sky, trying to beguile her son into flight. She called to him, called to his father to come and help. "Don't worry about the food, Temujin," I said down to him, "there's a blanke of flowers just waiting for you to fly over!" He turned from the sound of one to the other of the two women in his life, and politely ignored us both.

At last she came in to the aerie, obviously irritable. She pounded he food with her talons in a telling gesture that she gave it reluctantly. Temujin was upset but waited patiently for her temper to subside. His calm patience infuriated her and she flung herself away, shouting to her mate to follow her. Temujin tucked into the food hungrily. As he dozed in the afternoon sun, I sat on my ledge and watched him.

Soon he would fly high in the freedom of the skies, his wings against the clouds. He would be an eagle that would look straight into the sun. He was favored by the gods. The understanding between his mother and me had transcended the confines of eagle and human. How could I ask for more?

When his mother alighted again, he moved over to her and she nuzzled him, not angry anymore, giving him the long, searching looks of yearning she had showered on him as a baby. They cawed and grunted huskily at each other. He rubbed his neck against hers, pressing closer, as though trying to transfer some of her indomitable courage to his inexperienced frame.

They stayed like this for a long time, she watching him fondly as he stretched out his wings, one after the other, letting the sun shine onto each feather with the wind riffling through them. She roused the feathers on his head and along the top of his wings.

Time after time we watched their clashes of will and their subsequent reconciliation, noting them as among the most tender and endearing things in eagle behavior.

It was late afternoon but the sky was clear, the wind consistently strong. Temujin straightened to his full height, all imperial eagle, and moved to the edge of the aerie, looking round him as if consciously taking leave of his birthplace.

His parents circled nearer as he stretched his head into the wind toward the far-off peaks. He saw the freedom of the sky, his world, beckoning. He heard his parents above him. Then, with breathtaking suddenness, he answered the call of both.

At first he was inexpert. Drunk with the rapture of movement, he rolled and spiraled as he hit the updraughts and did not know what to make of them. The heights frightened him, and he flew along near the escarpment. The intoxication of it all caught at his body, and very soon he discovered that if he spread his wings and kept them rigid, the wind did all sorts of wonderful things for him. He found that it was quite unnecessary to flap at all to gain height. He experimented with his long primaries, the fingers with which he could command the wind. He used his tail. He soon made it look wondrously easy. His innate control and grace took on the joyous abandon of the young, and there was about him a joie de vivre, spinning him up, whirling him around in wild adventure.

They flew together, mother and son, father nearby, conscious of his responsibility, and oh! so proud, as they winged away out of sight, to leave to us nothing but summer clouds rising in gleaming white now, against the sky.

Filming a Legendary Old Eagle and Her Family

A thing of beauty is a joy forever;
Its loveliness increases; it will
Never pass into nothingness . . .
                    KEATS

I thought her hurt as she stood waiting in the valley. Never having seen the eagle this far down before, I went toward her. Half jumping, half flying from boulder to boulder, she kept just ahead of me, enjoying herself.

When we reached the plain, I sat on a tall rock, waiting for Arthur, and she stood just above me, cawing restlessly as if trying to find an explanation for the change in heart that brought her down to meet me. "You and your love," she seemed to say, "look what they have done to me." I called out to her, "Do you know Siegfried Sassoon?" She watched me intently, her head on one side, lovely in the morning—so lovely that I told her:

> Everyone suddenly burst out singing
> And I was filled with such delight
> As prisoned birds must find in freedom
> Winging wildly across the white
> Orchards and dark green fields; on; on; and out of
>   sight.

Everyone's voice was suddenly lifted
And beauty came like the setting sun.
My heart was shaken with tears; and horror
Drifted away . . . O but everyone
Was a bird; And the song was wordless; the singing
    will never be done . . .

It said everything and, unsteady as it was, my voice seemed to reassure her. She stood peaceably rousing her feathers. As Arthur came into view, she flapped and rose into the air. He shook his head, "I should be used to it by now!"

At the gully she came straight down, fluid and elegant as ever, a majestic bird allowing no concessions because of a bond between us.

"Where is he," I called.

He stood on a rock jutting over the top of the gully, straighter than his parents, as yet unbowed by the cares of adulthood. The mountain fell into place about him, the browns and gold of rock and grass merging with his colors.

In my gladness I scrambled up eagerly to him, naïvely expecting him to welcome me, to wait for my whistle, forgetting that this was a Temujin no longer bound to the aerie. He had spread his wings.

He watched my approach. This was the human he had always known, but the rules on the aerie had nothing to do with the new set he had inherited with his independence. I had hugged him often, carried him home, sat with him to comfort the wild beating of a terrified heart. But all that had been before he could fly.

He was puzzled, and torn. However, a powerful, ingrained instinct told him that humans—even this one he knew so well—were things of danger, and that his wings were meant to carry him away from them.

I sat halfway up the gully, as confused as he was. Until now I had not thought much beyond the delight at seeing him each week. Now I realized what I had known as fact, what all eagles had known since time began. It is man that is the "single greatest destroyer of the wild." My sharing of his life for a few months would fade from his recollection. The trust freely given in babyhood would give way to the dominant instinct of a hunter. It already had. And I would not want him to be different.

156

My heart turned over as he copied his mother's endearing habit of moving from foot to foot as though relying, as she did, on my knowing how close to come without making him fly away. His mother dropped down beside him, tossing her head with arrogant pride.

"Yes," I confessed. "He is truly splendid."

At last he leaned into the wind and glided along, his speckled wings flashing in the sun as they lazily guided his course.

Temujin the eaglet, now eagle, was lost to me.

> *In Nature there are neither rewards nor*
> *punishments — there are consequences . . .*
>
> INGERSOLL

Arthur wanted to film the two females, eagle and human, against the skyline, so he stayed on the plain. When the sun reached the rock face the filming would begin.

He shot thousands of feet of film, unique, gemlike sequences of an eagle family that would make a film on their own, but a great many of which had to be left out of the twenty-five-minute documentary film that has won him over half a dozen international awards. I wrote script after script, but each week brought something different, some facet of our life with the eagles that cried out for inclusion. This necessitated linkup shots and a change in the story, and eventually the script had to be matched to the particular episodes selected from the storehouse of film amassed by Arthur.

Patiently, Arthur set about filming what was required. He was a dedicated artist every moment of the time, seeing through his lens the friendship of the mother eagle and me, and my love for the family growing steadily. He angled his camera from impossible positions, while he staved off the wind and unexpected visits from the female eagle. When Temujin floundered away and was lost, he recorded the dramatic rescue and the return home under appalling conditions.

Arthur has done more rock climbing than I—my only experience being the Bell. He roped up always because he was burdened with photographic equipment and is not, as I am, exhilarated by heights. Mountaineers and ornithologists would perhaps shudder at my ropework that got Arthur down to the hide, and the hide we used. But both proved successful! Arthur came out of it unharmed, despite my unorthodox way of belaying him.

We had many problems—the wind, the eagles and the long drop below us. Arthur, heavily laden, went over the edge knowing that nothing was between him and the rocks below except the eagle and me arguing above him. And, with Arthur on the end of the rope, my two hands occupied, I had to take my chances with eagles and wind, feeling Arthur swaying against the rock face as he wondered how I was faring and whether my hands would remain firm against the onslaught of gale and eagle. Trying to position the hide in the howling wind, to control the whipping sail blown at right angles to the rock one minute, collapsing around us on the narrow ledge the next, was a nightmare. An icy blast was always in our faces, our eyes were never free of grit.

Arthur had to match light and weather. Temujin would only grow up once, and it was not always possible to repeat something beautiful or dramatic. The set was a rugged mountain and the vast sky, with no other lighting than that provided by the elements. The eagle film star could not be directed or learn any lines. She was not temperamental, just an unconfined creature of the wild, with no notion of obeying anyone. We had to await the eagles' pleasure in all things. We were slaves to them and the wind.

Arthur did not hide his doubt that the eagle would take food from me, but he knew that I could often persuade an old eagle actress to a particular stage for action shots. She and I raced about the mountain, and if Arthur saw the two of us presenting pleasing photographic possibilities he never hesitated to say so. Quite casually he would ask, "Do you think you and Mum could do that again?" "That" could be anything from offering the food on the edge of the rim, a near-miss with a talon or making my way along to the defended aerie, to a version of hide-and-seek among the summit rocks. He set up his camera and waited. Often I feared for his safety, and for Peter's, all of us knowing "the bright eye of danger."

Contributing our respective ideas, we were a well-knit team, though our minds looked for different rewards in our mountain adventure.

I considered that a lovely sweep of the mountain should be added to the film to give an essential feeling of vastness. Arthur heaved his camera on the long walk, then picked out a spur, saying,

"Okay, it's your idea, start running. . . ." And round I went, through crevices, into valleys, up slopes, until he signaled that it was the shot required.

For the skyline shot, with Arthur on the plain and me high above him on the escarpment edge, we would be out of range for easy communication, so we had arranged a sign language. It sounded straightforward. I was to walk along, as always, and stand with the food above the aerie. And, as always, the mother eagle seeing me there would follow me, fly over me, and Arthur's camera would pick up the sequence.

I looked across to the eagle rocks where all three of them sat placidly watching me as I waited for the mother's rush at me. It did not occur. And then I realized why. The aerie, since Temujin had left it, had lost its importance. They did not care whether I was there or not.

I could not see Arthur; he was lost somewhere on the plain amidst the conglomeration of boulders and bushes. Nor had we arranged any signs, anyway, that would cover this new turn of events. Arthur had changed his original position.

"Where are you?" I shouted, not able to pinpoint his whereabouts. Though he shouted "Here!" the sound could have come from anywhere on the plain. An extraordinary conversation ensued, with question and answer echoing and eddying into the strong wind between us. Sentences in tumbling jumps became the lines of a roundelay. It was quite uncanny not being able to see him.

"What—shall—I—do—with—this?" I shouted, bursting my lungs. I held up the food and waited for his reply.

His "Look—out!" came on a gust of wind too late to warn me as the eagle was on me, making for the rabbit in my upstretched hand. You never miss a trick, I thought, as I automatically ducked. The eagles' earlier serenity had relaxed my caution and I was too near the edge.

I saw the maw of the sheer drop opening beneath me. As I clung to the slight hold I had grabbed, shaken by the suddenness of it all, the food disappeared into the depths below me.

It seemed a lifetime before I heard Arthur's voice raised urgently from among the bushes against the base of the rock face. "Are you all right?" he asked. He was scratched, his clothes were torn by thorns and vines, but though he could give me no help, his encouragement brought movement back into my limbs and I started to haul myself up.

Arthur picked up the abandoned food, and in response to his request and now that my legs no longer felt like jelly, I let down the belaying rope. He obviously had more confidence in me than I had in myself.

The mother drifted backward and forward, interested in the proceedings. She had seen all this before, was quite accustomed to the rope as she was to seeing Arthur on the end of it and me sitting at the top. But her casual interest quickened into vehement indignation when she saw on the end of the rope not Arthur but the food! She took her impatience out on me and showered me with a torrent of talon flicks, at the same time making concerted dives at the ascending food.

"When you have it," Arthur shouted, "and I have had time to get back to my camera, go right to the edge again and give it to her there."

You just have to admire people like that!

But the time was to come when watching the film would fill me with yearning, when seeing the mountain on the screen would be heartache, and the eagles, heartbreak. Yet the pure joy of being there, of being part of the film, carried me with my eagle friends to the stars.

Last Days With My Eagle Friends

We must be free or die . . .
WORDSWORTH

Lightning daggered over the mighty ranges, and above the camp the moon was suffused with haze as it glowed through the rain-filmed clouds.

The eagle was etched into her mountain, the proud old crusader vividly part of the summit outline. My time with her family would soon be over and I savored her beauty caught up in the moonlight.

I had to leave them. I felt strongly that I would only be doing them a disservice by coming back again and again to break down further their natural reserve against humans. Not all humans would be as we were. And yet I knew, too, that sometime I would have to go to the mountain if just to get a glimpse of them.

I have since returned, forgoing friendship and recognition because I believed I must for their sake. I climbed the mountain from the buzzard side, leaving in the early hours of the morning, leaving my gift of food, and was down again, watching them through binoculars, by the time dawn broke. Thus I have soared with them still, but from afar, the food unconnected with me. And

161

thus it was that one year I knew with a heavy heart that my old friend would not return.

The moon lowered and the sun took over the mountain as I lay in my sleeping bag, listening to the storm roll away and looking around me at this eagle country. I felt a finality about the mountain putting on its best face. I had known it in all weathers—beset by gales, flooded with the sun, mantled with snow, ariot with flowers. It had known my despair and elation; it had been part of my miracles; it had offered some protection against the elements, seen me cold and numb, and had given me strange but real comfort. It was home to my eagles and, like them, it was known and loved. Like them, too, I would not forget it.

The eagle was not alone. Hers was the silhouette I had seen. But now the light caught at Temujin and his father. The eagle family was not to be outdone by the mountain. They, too, were out to please me.

"Saku Bona!" is the Zulu's greeting. And I shouted it to her as she swung into place above the gully. "I see you, old miracle." Zooming over, her answer could only be "I see you," as she gave a wonderful display of ostentatious gully normality. And I laughed aloud at the pure joy of her.

Except for my heartache, that day was one of pure enchantment. I stumbled after Temujin each time he made a move boulder-hopping round our side of the mountain, I knowing just how close to go, and he unconcerned at my being there. He expended a great deal of energy in flying short distances, keeping close to the mountain. That he wanted to try out his wings was very obvious. Often he waited patiently until I caught up to him, while his mother flew patronizingly tolerantly above us, sometimes gliding in swiftly toward me but with no talon intentions. When we reached the blanket of flowers near the peak, with Temujin flying low over them to prevent him from venturing too near buzzard territory, his mother and I gently turned his course back. While he was on the ground I kept my back to the buzzard side of the mountain, and in the air his mother did the same. And how could he defy us both?

Later, his parents alighted on their special rock and Temujin circled uncertainly until he joined them on a smaller one nearby. I went toward them and, choosing my own rock, sat with my eagles gathered about me. How great was my love for them then. My whistle made Temujin swiftly lift his head to me, my voice inspired quick rejoinder from his mother, and my presence, though it seemed it would always bother him, was no longer as unwelcome to the father as it had once been.

How much I hated leaving them! Yet I knew I would never want to "tame" these wild, proud giants, even remotely. My remembrance of them—free, resplendent and mighty—would spill, rich in pictures, forever into mind. I would not want any compromise because of our friendship. I could only be richer for having known them; my world could only be better for having touched theirs.

I walked away from them, along the escarpment edge, not looking back, but I knew she flew above me. The farther I went from Temujin and his parents, the more difficult I found it to believe that good-bye is anything but a tearing thing that strangles you.

When she saw that I held food in my hand, she called out as though in surprise, and raced immediately to the summit, hanging there, an eagle owning the sky. I caught my breath. A friendship strong enough to know what I wanted, and to give it to me without question!

I held the food up and saw the glory of her as she rushed down in exhilarating, untroubled abandon, loving every moment of this tingling flight that called on every reserve in her except the necessity for caution; and giving, at the end of it, food without the possibility of danger. I could see the power and strength of her, and the beauty of this, my eagle friend.

She took the food joyously and swept into the splendor of the sky, then did a tight circle over again as if in quick thanks. This time she did not bargain, nor was the food alms. The gift, and the accepting of it, were inseparable, gracious and proud—as strong and unconditional as the voluntary bonds of our friendship.

> *The benediction of these covering heavens*
> *Falls on their heads like dew . . .*
> SHAKESPEARE

In the hush of late afternoon the sun filtered over the ridges as it melted into the Drakensberg range, and thunder came like the boom of a gong. The wind fretted and fumed, chasing the storm clouds back from our mountain. The plain was flooded with light and the high peak of the summit was like the candle flame I had first seen.

The mother flew toward the butcher's block and I followed, then stopped as I saw her leave the food there before returning to her mate and son. For a while she stood with them as I drew closer, then she left her rock and, after calling out to me as she circled, returned to her family, continuing her circling above them. Tighter and tighter became her flying, as though she was weaving a funnel that would draw them to her.

Responding to her magnetism, her mate rose and joined her. They floated patiently, not hurrying the eaglet, and even I, earthbound, could feel the call of the wind coursing through me as though I, too, would be pulled up to them.

Temujin looked over at me, then up to his parents, a glorious young eagle more than ready, now, to tackle the heights. He did so with an ardent sweep of his wings, choosing an updraught that carried him straight in a continuous flow to where they waited. Gone was the hesitancy that had kept him near the mountain. He rose higher and higher, followed by the adults. Pride and satisfaction radiated from them as they watched the progress of their precious heir.

You are well named, my small friend, I thought as I watched him revel in his wings. Now that your boyhood is almost behind you, your strong, invincible nomad of a namesake will soon give of his characteristics: Genghis, meaning wide, encompassing; and Khan, the chief, the great conqueror. But now, to me, he was still little Temujin.

I turned to make my way down the gully, beset with loneliness. The eagles' very beauty intensified my desolation. They turned to come back. The tiny specks changed into eagle forms limned in the gold of the sunset, and I could hear a haunting baby-call echoing on the harping currents that held Temujin aloft.

Then he was over me in a lopsided salute as he tilted over the spur. He spiraled and again made a long dive toward me. He may have been showing off, but how beautifully he was doing it! He planed up to his parents to complete the trilogy in the clouds, confident and eager in the joy of the sky that was his.

Temujin, the Rider of Heaven!

Down on the plain I plodded among the rocks to join Arthur. "Here comes your friend," he said quietly.

The great mother eagle came to bid me farewell alone. She arrived in a breathtaking swoop, her wings scything the gold of the evening into slivers of feathered gilt. She alighted on a rock in front of my path and called constantly as I went slowly toward her. And the endearing restlessness was there, the muted cawing that made my heart spill over and churned me up inside.

I wanted to tell her a host of things—to explain how I felt about her; to thank her, and say I would never forget her. But the words choked in me at the sight of her standing there. She waited, alternately looking at me and her mate and son, and then took off, rising wonderfully fast. She glided back, strangely untroubled at being so far down the mountain. She seemed loath to go. And I hoped she never would; hoped, too, that she would never miss me as much as the emptiness that was draining me.

I walked on away from her as she swung into a thermal and joined her family. And my love for them rose up in me like a tide.

They soared around me, beautiful, poignant, and I was stirred with the deep joy I always felt for them, but also with an overwhelming sense of loss. Blindly, I followed their graceful course, three eagles who had given me so much, weaving their splendid poetry against the Drakensberg clouds—wild, remote, magnificent.

Then I went down the mountain, bereft.

Photo credits